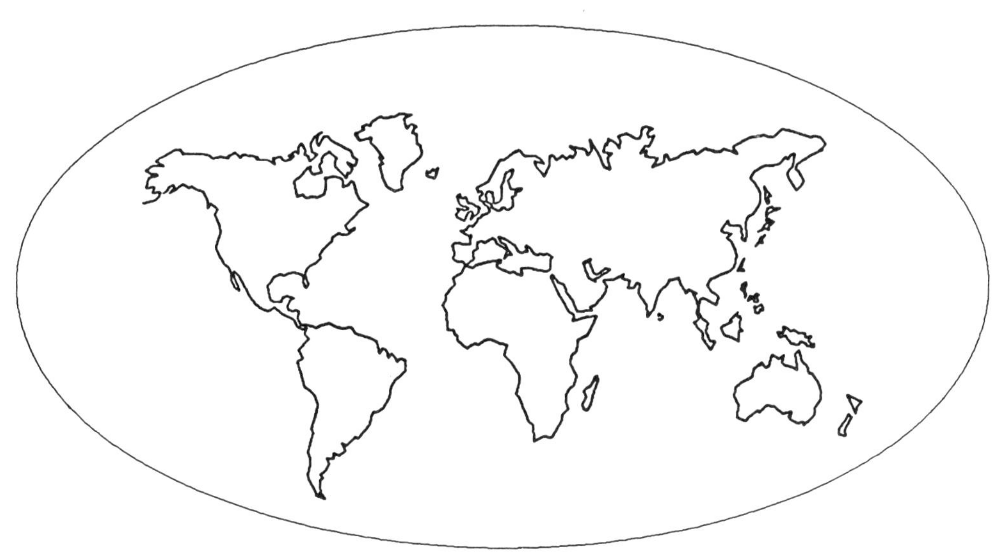

WORLD TAPESTRY TODAY

World touring exhibition organized by the American Tapestry Alliance, Chiloquin, Oregon, U.S.A., in collaboration with the Victorian Tapestry Workshop, Melbourne, Australia.

The exhibition is a featured event of the International Tapestry Symposium, "Tapestry Today" sponsored by the Victorian Tapestry Workshop as part of the Australian Bicentennial celebration.

Melbourne • Chicago • Memphis • New York • Heidelberg • Stuttgart • Aubusson

1988 - 89 VENUES

Meat Market Craft Centre
Melbourne, Australia
May–June 1988

The Chicago Public Library Cultural Center
Chicago, Illinois, U.S.A.
July–August 1988

Bell•Ross Gallery
Memphis, Tennessee, U.S.A.
September–October 1988

Scheuer Tapestry Gallery
New York, New York, U.S.A.
October–November 1988

Max Berk Textile Museum
Heidelberg, Germany
December 1988–January 1989

Stuttgart City Hall
Stuttgart, Germany
February–March 1989

Musée départemental de la tapisserie
Centre Culturel et Artistique Jean Lurçat
Aubusson, France
April–June 1989

Library of Congress
Catalog Card Number: 88-70295

ISBN 0-945858-01-9

American Tapestry Alliance
HC 63 Box 570-D
Chiloquin, Oregon 97624

Printed in U.S.A.

TABLE OF CONTENTS

FOREWORD

The end of the eighties is bound to become a turning point for international tapestry. The majority of the questions posed at the Melbourne Conference come at a time when, in many countries, tapestry makers have a new outlook on concepts developed by tapestry in the past few years.

As a matter of fact, less than thirty years separate us from the first Lausanne Biennal where Jean Lurçat, with the help of a daring municipality, was able to realize his dream of a gathering of the whole world of tapestry on a regular basis.

This event was quite a breakthrough for tapestry which received a world-wide consecration and a remarkable recognition from the art market. At the time this development occured, it was also the concretisation of a great danger: it showed that a fundamental renewal was occurring in the entire world.

Between 1964 and 1987, we have witnessed a true explosion of the definition of an art which was able to gain independance from painting, incorporate other textile techniques, expand its range of basic materials, reflect on its history, its sources and its millenary memory.

Tapestry gained by reflecting on itself but was on the verge of losing its identity by integrating the approaches of other disciplines: painting, sculpture, photography and the ideas of the great art movements: minimalism, poor art, conceptual art.

Today the time has come for a new consideration: the woven tapestry was able to recognize its extra-European sources: Coptic and pre-Columbian textures. It has also found artists capable of combining the Oriental traditions (k'osseu) and the occidental development of European workshops. It is aware of William Morris' message and of the Arts and Crafts Movement. Finally it realized that it could perfectly integrate itself in the newly-born post-modern period where artisans' traditions meet with computers and where photography and video can be the starting point of contemporary image-making as strong as 18th century cartoon image-making.

SUITE

La fin des années quatre-vingt doit constituer le moment d'un tournant important pour la tapisserie internationale. L'ensemble des interrogations posées au cours de la conférence de Melbourne interviennent au moment où, dans de nombreux pays un regard nouveau des créateurs se pose sur les concepts développés par la tapisserie des dernières années.

En effet, moins de trente ans nous séparent de la première Biennale de Lausanne où Jean Lurçat, aidé par une municipalité entreprenante a pu réaliser le rêve d'une manifestation regulière qui réunisse le monde entier de la tapisserie.

Cette decision a été à la fois une grande chance pour la tapisserie, qui a reçu ainsi une consecration mondiale et une reconnaissance éclatante du marché de l'art, mais aussi, compte tenu de l'époque où elle est intervenue, la concrétisation d'un grand danger: celui de montrer qu'un renouvellement fondamental était en train d'intervenir dans le monde entier.

De 1964 a 1987 on a pu ainsi assister à une véritable explosion de la définition d'un art qui a su prendre son indépendance de la peinture, faire alliance avec d'autres techniques textiles, renouveler ses matériaux, réfléchir sur son histoire, ses sources et sa mémoire millénaire. La tapisserie y a gagné en reflexion sur elle-même, mais a failli perdre son identité en intégrant les approches d'autres disciplines: peintures, sculpture, photographie et les idées des grands courants artistiques: minimalisme, art pauvre, art conceptuel.

Aujourd'hui le temps est venu d'une nouvelle reconsidération: la tapisserie tissée a su reconnaitre ses sources extra-europeennes: tissus coptes et précolombiens. Elle a su trouver des créateurs capables de créer une alliance entre les traditions orientales (le k'osseu) et le développement occidental des ateliers européens. Elle a pris conscience du message essentiel de William Morris et de l'Arts and Crafts movement. Elle a enfin compris qu'elle pouvait parfaitement s'intégrer à l'époque post-moderne qui vient de naitre où les traditions artisanales rencontrent l'ordinateur et où la photographie et la video peuvent servir de point de départ à une imagerie contemporaine aussi forte que celle des cartons du XIIIeme siècle. En confrontant

VORWORT

Das Ende der achtziger Jahre ist im Begriff, ein bedeutender Wendepunkt für die internationale Tapisserie zu werden. Die Mehrzahl der Fragen, die bei der Melbourner Konferenz gestellt wurden, kommen zu einem Zeitpunkt, wenn viele Weber in zahlreichen Ländern eine neue Einstellung zur Tapisserie der vergangenen Jahre gewonnen haben.

Es sind weniger als 30 jahre vergangen, seitdem Jean Lurçat mit der kühnen Hilfe einer Gemeinde bei der ersten Lausanner Biennale seinen Traum erfüllen konnte, die ganze Tapisseriewelt zu vereinigen.

Dieses Ereignis war ein grosser Erfolg für die Tapisserie, die dadurch weltweiten Applaus und Anerkennung in Kunstkreisen erntete. Das bedeutete, dass auf der ganzen Welt eine Regenerierung stattfand.

Zwischen 1964 und 1987 gab es unzählige neue Definitionen einer Kunst, die nun unabhängig von der Malerei war. Es wurde mit neuen Textilverfahren und Materialien experimentiert und man betrachtete die Geschichte und tausendjährige Tradition der Webkunst mit neuen Augen.

Die Tapisserie machte Fortschritte auf ihrer Reise in die Vergangenheit, aber sie geriet in eine Identitätskrise, indem sie sich an Gestaltungspraktiken der Malerei, Skulptur und Photographie orientierte. Die Tapisserie borgte auch von Kunstrichtungen wie Minimalismus, "Art Pauvre" und "Concept Art".

Es ist nun höchste Zeit, dass man im Tapisserieweben auch auf die aussereuropäischen Quellen aufmerksam wird: die koptischen und vorkolumbianischen Webarbeiten. In europaischen Ateliers verbinden manche Künstler die orientalische Tradition (K'osseu) mit Stilelementen des Westens. Die Tapisseriebewegung ist sich der Bedeutung von William Morris' Werk und der "Arts and Crafts Movement" bewusst. Die Tapisserie hat endlich ihren Platz in der postmodernen Epoche gefunden—eine Epoche, in der das Kunsthandwerk auf Computer trifft und wo die Photographie und das Video einen Ansatzpunkt zu aktueller Gestaltung bilden, die eine ebenso starke Ausstrahlung besitzt wie die Kartons des achtzehnten Jahrhunderts.

By comparing Raphael's cartoons with Franz Kafka's photographic portraits, Jan Hladik comes up with contemporary answers to an old question. By looking into the profound nature of the k'osseu, Souk Hi Li is able to synthesize the Orient and the Occident. Stefan Poplawski, Marcel Marois and Ruth Scheuer take an interest in current political and ecological events, reinterprete the images of nature and magazines and are therefore able to reflect major problems of their time in their tapestries. They rediscover the tradition of tapestry as a mirror of time and history.

Michel Thomas
January 1988

Michel Thomas is the editor of "Textile/Art". He is also the co-publisher of *Textile Art* with Skira/Rizzoli. Mr. Thomas organized the international exhibition "Fibre-Art" at the Museum of Decorative Arts in Paris in 1985. His writings have brought him international reknown.

les cartons de Raphaël et les portraits photographiques de Franz Kafka, Jan Hladik apporte des réponses actuelles à une question ancienne. En se penchant sur la nature profonde du k'osseu, Souk Hi Li sait faire la synthèse de l'Orient et de l'Occident. En s'intéressant à l'actualité politique et écologique, en réinterpretant les images de la nature et des magazines, Stefan Poplawski, Marcel Marois ou Ruth Scheuer insèrent la tapisserie dans les grands problèmes de leur époque et retrouvent les traditions de la tapisserie, miroir du temps et de l'Histoire.

Michel Thomas
Janvier 1988

Michel Thomas est le "Directeur de la Publication," "Textile/Art." Il a aussi publié *Art Textile* en collaboration avec Skira/Rizzoli, 1985. M. Thomas a organisé l'exposition internationale "Fibre-Art" qui s'est déroulée au Musée des Arts Décoratifs à Paris en 1985. Les écrits sur la tapisserie et l'art des fibres de M. Thomas lui ont apporté une renommée internationale.

Im Vergleich von Raphaels Kartons mit Franz Kafkas Photoportraits hat Jan Hladik auf eine alte Frage eine zeitgemässe Antwort gefunden. Souk Hi Li vereinigt Orient und Okzident durch Experimente mit dem K'osseu. Durch ihr Interesse an aktuellen politischen und ökologischen Ereignissen können Stefan Poplawski, Marcel Marois und Ruth Scheuer Elemente aus der Natur und aus Zeitschriften neu interpretieren und daher wichtige aktuelle Probleme in ihren Webarbeiten reflektieren. Sie beleben die Tradition der Tapisserie als ein Spiegel der Zeit und der Geschichte.

Michel Thomas
Januar 1988

Michel Thomas ist der Herausgeber von "Textile/Art". Er ist auch ein Co-Author von Textile Art, dass durch Skira/Rizzoli veröffentlicht wird. Er hat die Internationale Faserkunstausstellung organisiert, die im Museum der dekorativen Künste 1985 in Paris stattfand. Michel Thomas ist als Schriftsteller über Web-und Faserkunst international bekannt.

INTRODUCTION

The "World Tapestry Today" exhibition was curated by the American Tapestry Alliance to provide two conferences on two continents ("International Tapestry Symposium," Melbourne, Australia and the Handweavers Guild of America's "Convergence," Chicago, U.S.A.) graphic examples of the breadth of tapestry around the globe of today's leading tapestry makers as well as those aspiring new talents. Interest in this exhibition also prompted scheduling the three venues in Europe: the Max Berk Textil Museum, Heidelberg, Germany; the Stuttgart City Hall, Stuttgart, Germany; and the Musee de la tapisserie, Centre Culturel et Artistique Jean Lurçat, Aubusson, France.

The American Tapestry Alliance is grateful to the Victorian Tapestry Workshop for accepting our proposal to have "World Tapestry Today" be a featured part of their symposium, "Tapestry Today." Their collaboration in planning for the exhibition in Melbourne, Australia as part of the Australian Bicentennial celebration has been instrumental in focusing attention on tapestry and tapestry makers around the world.

After two decades of what has been called the "fiber explosion," the tapestry makers, who quietly studied and pursued their medium without feeling the need to compromise their technical training for the sake of being avant garde, finally have their chance to be seen. The fact that several hundred of these artists convened at the Melbourne symposium is a clear indication that this ancient art form still survives. Although many may have thought it on the "endangered" list, it is evident that not only does it survive, but many individual, young and talented artists have discovered the passion for this art form. Their "statements" throughout this book attest to that passion.

The American Tapestry Alliance hopes to discover even more artists-craftsmen for future exhibitions, as well as to locate more venues interested in exhibiting this timeless and noble art. We feel confident on both counts, for in the brief time of one year we were not able to reach all artists of the world in this media and regretfully had to decline a number of venue requests because of prior scheduling.

As mentioned by Michel Thomas in his Introduction, ". . . that Jean Lurçat with the help of a daring municipality realized his dream of a gathering of the world of tapestry," we hope "World Tapestry Today" will be a continuation of that dream and that there are other daring municipalities, be they city/states, townships or corporations willing to help in seeing that this world of tapestry continues to grow.

AVANT-PROPOS

L'exposition "Le Monde de la Tapisserie Aujourd'hui" a été montée par l'Alliance Américaine de la Tapisserie pour produire deux conférences sur deux continents, (Symposium International de la Tapisserie", à Melbourne en Australie et la "Réunion" des Compagnons Tisseurs d'Amérique, à Chicago aux Etats-Unis). Des exemples graphiques seront montrés des tapisseries produites par les leaders actuels de la tapisserie ainsi que par de jeunes et talentueux artistes. L'intérêt suscité par cette exposition nous a également incité à la transporter en Europe: elle y sera montrée trois fois au Musée Textile de Max Berk, Heidelberg, Allemagne, au Hall de Stuttgart à Stuttgart, Allemagne et au Musée de la Tapisserie, au Centre Culturel et Artistique Jean Lurçat, à Aubusson en France.

L'Alliance Américaine de la Tapisserie remercie l'Atelier Victorien de la Tapisserie d'avoir accepté notre proposition d'avoir la "Tapisserie dans le Monde Aujourd'hui" présentée lors de leur symposium, "la Tapisserie Aujourd'hui". Leur collaboration au planning de l'exposition à Melbourne, Australie, comme part des festivités du bicentennial australien a permis d'attirer l'attention sur la tapisserie et sur les tapissiers du monde.

Aprés deux décades de ce qu'on a appelé l'explosion des fibres, les tapissiers qui étudiaient dans le calme et s'adonnaient à leur art sans ressentir le besoin de sacrifier leur acquis technique au desir d'être avant-garde ont enfin la possibilité d'être reconnus. Le fait que plusieurs centaines de ces artistes se soient réunis lors du symposium de Melbourne, indique clairement que cette ancienne forme d'art est encore actuelle. Bien que beaucoup l'aient deja couchée sur la liste des espèces en voie de disparition, il est évident qu'elle ne se contente pas seulement de survivre mais que beaucoup de jeunes artistes talentueux se sont découvert une passion pour cette forme d'art. Leur message dans ce livre est le fruit de cette passion.

L'Alliance Américaine pour la Tapisserie espère encore plus découvrir d'artistes et d'artisans pour des expositions futures ainsi que de trouver des lieux ou exposer cette forme d'art noble et hors du temps. Nous avons confiance dans ces deux recherches car dans la brêve période d'une année nous n'avons pas pu toucher tous les artistes du monde de cette forme d'art et avons malheureusement oû refuser des possibilités d'exposition à cause d'engagements préalables.

Ainsi que le mentionne Michel Thomas dans son Introduction, ". . . que Jean Lurçat avec l'aide d'une municipalité entreprenante a réalisé son rêve d'une réunion du monde de la tapisserie", nous espérons que le "Monde de la Tapisserie Aujourd'hui" servira à poursuivre ce rêve at qu'il y aura d'autres municipalités entreprenantes, que ce soit des villes, des états ou des entreprises désireuses d'aider à faire en sorte que le monde de la tapisserie continue de s'élargir.

EINLEITUNG

Die Ausstellung "Welttapisserie Heute" wurde von der Amerikanischen Tapisserievereinigung organisiert, um zwei Tagungen auf zwei verschiedenen Kontinenten (das "Internationale Tapisseriesymposium" in Melbourne, Australien, und die "Convergence" der Handwebervereinigung in Chicago, U.S.A.) einen Einblick in die weltweite Tapisseriebewegung zu gewähren und die Werke der führenden etablierten Tapisserieweber sowie die Werke junger talentierter Künstler auszustellen. Das wachsende Interesse veranlasste drei Ausstellungsstätten in Europa, diese Ausstellung in ihr Programm aufzunehmen: das Max Berk Textilmuseum in Heidelberg, das Stuttgarter Rathaus und das Musee de la Tapisserie, Centre Culturel et Artistique Jean Lurçat in Aubusson, Frankreich.

Die Amerikanische Tapisserievereinigung dankt der Leitung des Victoria Tapestry Workshops, daβ sie "Welttapisserie Heute" in ihr Symposium "Tapisserie Heute" einbezogen hat. Ihre Zusammenarbeit bei der Planung für die Ausstellung in Melbourne als Teil der australischen Zweihundertjahrfeier hat viel dazu beigetragen, die Aufmerksamkeit auf die Tapisserie und die Tapisserieweber der ganzen Welt zu lenken.

Nach zwei Jahrzehnten der sogenannten "Faserexplosion" haben viele Weber endlich die Gelegenheit, ihre Werke zu zeigen. Es handelt sich hauptsächlich um Weber, die in ihrem Medium still vor sich hin gewirkt haben ohne ihre Fähigkeiten zu Gunsten der Avantgarde zu kompromittieren. Die Tatsache, daβ Hunderte dieser Künstler am Melbourner Symposium teilnahmen, ist ein klares Zeichen, daβ diese alte Kunstform noch überlebt. Obwohl es einige Zweifel gab, ist es nun erwiesen, daβ diese Kunst nicht nur überlebt hat, sondern daβ viele jung talentierte Künstler in dieser Kunstform mit Begeisterung tätig sind. Ihre Aussagen in diesem Buch bestätigen es.

Die Amerikanische Tapisserievereinigung hofft, weitere Künstler für künftige Ausstellungen zu entdecken und weitere Ausstelllungsorte ausfindig zu machen, die bereit wären, diese zeitlose und edle Kunst auszustellen. Wir sind diesbezüglich sehr zuversichtlich. In der kurzen Zeitspanne von einem Jahr waren wir nicht einmal in der Lage, alle Künstler in diesem Medium zu erreichen und muβten bedauerlicherweise aus Zeitgründen Angebote von mehreren Ausstellungsstätten ablehnen.

Wie schon Michel Thomas in seiner Einleitung erwähnt ". . . daβ Jean Lurçat mit der Unterstützung einer kühnen Gemeinde seinen Traum verwirklichen konnte, die Tapisseriewelt zu vereinigen", so hoffen wir, daβ "Welttapisserie Heute" eine Fortsetzung dieses Traums bildet und daβ es andere Quellen gibt (Städte, Gemeinden, Staaten oder Private Firmen), die ihre Unterstützung für den Fortschritt in der Tapisserie anbieten.

The American Tapestry Alliance has, since its inception in 1982, tried to encourage the new tapestry makers of our era and help give them recognition through exhibitions such as this one. It has scrupulously followed anonymous selection by jury panels, who judge on an individual basis, for all of its competitions. This procedure was adopted in order to give all talents as equal an opportunity as possible, whether they were members or not. The membership has benefitted by growth and enthusiasm from this policy.

The directors of the American Tapestry Alliance and Victorian Tapestry Workshop are indebted to the panel of jurors they selected for accepting the task of viewing seven pounds of slides.

We chose Jenny Zimmer, Dean of Art and Design at the Chisholm Institute of Technology, Caulfield East, Victoria as the Australian juror; Marcel Marois, professor of Tapestry, Painting and Drawing at the University of Quebec and University of Laval, Quebec, Canada as the North American juror; Mary Farmer, Head of Tapestry Studio, Royal College of Art, London, England, and Paul Risch, Director, Ecole Nationale d-Art Decoratif d'Aubusson, France as the European jurors. Their expertise in the fields of art and tapestry is evident in the selections made for "World Tapestry Today."

Each juror scored each submitted work for originality, design, use of color and technique. The scores were then compiled by computer and the highest scored works selected for the exhibition. To be as impartial as possible, the jurors were urged to "pass" the work if they recognized it, in an effort to eliminate any temptations of national preferences. We are greatly indebted to their dedicated effort. The summary at the end of the catalogue will give some indication of the vast task they performed.

I do hope the viewer of this collection either at the exhibitions or in this catalogue will enjoy the works of these very active worldwide talents and will join in our search for the "World's Choice" award by casting your ballot for the tapestry you enjoy the most. Ballot cards are available at each venue and in each catalogue.

Jim Brown
Director,
American Tapestry Alliance

L'Alliance Américaine pour la Tapisserie, depuis sa fondation en 1982 a essayé d'encourager les nouveaux tapissiers de notre temps et à aider à les faire connaitre lors d'exposiitons comme celle-ci. Elle a scrupuleusement suivi une selection anonyme par plusieurs membres d'un jury qui jugent individuellement lors de chacun de ces concours. Cette procédure a été adoptée de façon à donner à tous les talents une chance égale qu'ils soient ou non membres de l'association. Cette politique nous a permis d'accroitre à la fois le nombre et l'enthousiasme de nos membres.

Les directeurs de l'Alliance Américaine pour la Tapisserie et de l'Atelier Victorien de Tapisserie sont très reconnaissants au jury qu'ils ont choisi d'avoir accepté la tâche de visionner sept livres de diapositives.

Nous avons choisi Jenny Zimmer, Dean of Art and Design de L'institut de Technologie de Chisholm, Caulfield East, Victoria comme jury Australien: Marcel Marois, professeur de tapisserie, peinture et dessin à l'Université de Québec et l'Université de Laval, Québec, Canada comme jury d'Amérique du Nord; Mary Farmer, Head of Tapestry Studio, Royal College of Art, Londres, Angleterre et Paul Risch, Directeur de l'Ecole Nationale d'Art Décoratif d'Aubusson, France comme jury européen. Leur expertise dans le domaine de l'art et de la tapisserie est évident dans leurs selections pour le "Monde de la Tapisserie Aujourd'hui".

Chaque jury a noté chaque œuvre soumise selon les critères d'originalité, conception, utilisation de la couleur et technique. Les notes ont été additionnées par ordinateur et les œuvres les mieux notées ont été sélectionnées pour l'exposition. Pour être aussi impartial que possible, on avait demandé au jury de ne pas noter une œuvre qu'ils auraient reconnue pour éliminer toute tentation de favoritisme. Nous leur sommes grandement redevable de leur effort. Le résumé à la fin du catalogue donnera l'idée de l'ampleur de la tâche qu'ils ont accomplie.

J'espère que quiconque verra cette collection, soit lors des expositions ou dans ce catalogue, appréciera les oeuvres de ces talents actifs du monde entier et se joindra à nous dans notre recherche de la récompense "du choix du monde" en votant pour la tapisserie qui lui plait le plus. Vous trouverez des bulletins de vote à chaque exposition et dans chaque catalogue.

Jim Brown
Directeur,
L'Alliance Américaine de la Tappisserie

Die Amerikanische Tapisserievereinigung hat seit ihrer Gründung 1982 die neuen Tapisserieweber unserer Zeit ermutigt und ihnen Anerkennung durch Ausstellungen wie diese verschafft. Die Bewerber für diese Ausstellung wurden anonym durch eine Jury von Sachverständigen gewählt. Auf diese Weise wurden allen Künstlern gleiche Chancen eingeräumt, ob sie nun Mitglieder waren oder nicht.

Die Leiter der Amerikanischen Tapisserievereinigung und des Victorian Tapisserieworkshops bedanken sich bei den Sachverständigen, die sich bereit erklärten, ca. sieben Pfund Lichtbilder zu beurteilen.

Die Jury bestand aus: Jenny Zimmer, Dekan für Kunst und Design am Chisholm Institut für Technologie, Caulfield East, Victoria, Australien; Marcel Marois, Professor für Tapisserie, Malerei und Zeichnen an der Universität von Quebec und Laval in Quebec, Kanada; Mary Farmer, Leiterin des Tapisseriestudios am Royal College of Art in London, und Paul Risch, Leiter des Ecole Nationale d'Art Decoratif d'Aubusson, Frankreich. Ihre Auswahl für "Welttapisserie Heute" ist ein Beweis ihrer Fähigkeiten und Sachkenntnis auf dem Gebiet der Kunst und der Tapisserie.

Die eingesandten Werke wurden nach folgenden Kriterien bewertet: Orginalität, Entwurf, Anwendung der Farbe und der Methode. Die Ergebnisse Wurden im Computer errechnet und die Werke mit der höchsten Bewertung für die Ausstellung ausgewählt. Um Bevorzugung zu vermeiden, wurden die Jurymitglieder gebeten, sich der Stimme zu enthalten, falls ihnen eins der Werke bekannt vorkam.

Wir bedanken uns bei ihnen für ihre Bemühungen. Die Zusammenfassung am Ende dieses Katalogs deutet an, welch eine ungeheure Aufgabe sie bewältigen muβten.

Ich hoffe, daβ der Betrachter beim Ausstellungsbesuch oder beim Durchblättern dieses Katalogs die Werke dieser talentierten Künstler aus aller Welt zu schätzen weiβ und uns dabei helfen wird, durch Ausfüllen der Stimmzettel das "Weltbeste Werk" zu ermitteln. Die Stimmzettel befinden sich in jedem Katalog und sind an jedem Ausstellungsort erhältlich.

Jim Brown
Direktor,
Amerikanische Tapisserievereinigung

WORLD TAPESTRY TODAY

A quarter of a century can be of little consequence to a process that has existed in sophisticated form for two—even three thousand years.

However, at a time when the pace of change in all aspects of living has been increasingly astonishing, and when, in the arts, the act of change alone; the simple fact of being different from before, is consistently lauded, the process of making woven tapestry seems, too, to have gone through radical re-thinking.

Time may well show that what seems to be major developments are in fact mere falters. Nevertheless 1962 was the year of tapestry's first major international exhibition so it is appropriate, a quarter of a century later, to look at tapestry today and to consider the changes.

I can recall, in 1958, a private moment of discovery when the surface of tapestry came alive. Today these discoveries may seem trivial and common place, but I remember a great silent excitement—a sneaking sense of guilt. As an apprentice I had tried out various warp materials, warp spacings and warp to weft ratios. But now, when weaving a small tapestry, I had woven a small scrap of seine cotton on top of a tiny passage of 'standard' woollen weft. I had been seeking a particular shade of near white but it was the surface contrast between the two materials that set thinking. Within an hour I had juxtaposed wefts of linen, jute, rayon, sewing threads, silk, and various 'on the spot' hand spinnings of woollen yarns. I had even tried lines of raised soumak knots and discreet tufts sprouting from the surface. And to be in direct contact with the changing surface I was weaving from the front of the upright loom (after ten years working from the back and using a mirror). I still have that tapestry, but it was some years before the real significance of that hour became clear to me.

My silence then was because I couldn't share the excitement with any of the only three tapestry weavers I knew who were a hundred miles north in Edinburgh. The reality was that around Europe and in other parts of the world there were many weavers busy poking in the same corners and asking similar questions.

My sense of guilt was because I was breaking 'the rules'—tapestry rules that had been thoroughly argued in my training—rules finally established after much struggle and resistance in French tapestry workshops just a decade or so earlier.

LA TAPISSERIE DANS LE MONDE D'AUJOURD'HUI

Un quart de siècle n'apporte pas grand changement à un procédé qui existe sous une forme sophistiquée depuis deux—ou même trois mille ans.

Cependant, à une epoque ou chaque aspect de notre vie change a une vitesse étonnante, surtout dans les arts où on loue le seul fait de changer ou de se montrer différent d'avant, la fabrication de la tapisserie tissée à la main semble elle-aussi être radicalement remise en question.

Le temps seul nous dira si nous avons affaire à des développements fondamentaux ou à de simples hésitations. Toutefois, la première exposition internationale de la tapisserie ayant eu lieu en 1962, il est normal que, 25 ans plus tard, nous nous intéressions à la tapisserie d'aujourd'hui et que nous examinions les transformations qu'elle subit.

Je n'ai pas oublié l'instant privilegié, en 1958, où j'ai senti que ma tapisserie prenait vie. Aujourd'hui, cette découverte me parait insignifiante et banale mais je me souviens encore d' avoir éprouvé un émoi profond et silencieux—un sentiment léger de culpabilité. Lorsque j'étais apprenti, j'avais essayé des chaînes de matières et d'espaces divers ainsi que des proportions variées entre la chaîne et la trame. Mais alors que je travaillais sur une petite tapisserie, j'avais tissé un petit bout de coton de Seine par dessus un morceau minuscule de trame en laine ordinaire. Je cherchais une teinte particulière de blanc cassé et le contraste entre la surface des deux élements me donna à réflechir. En moins d'une heure, je juxtaposai des trames de lin, jute, rayonne, fil à coudre, soie et divers écheveaux de laine que j'avais filés à la main. J'agrémentais aussi la surface de rangées de noeuds de soumac et de touffes discrétes. Afin d'avoir un contact direct avec la surface, je tissais de l'avant du métier à tisser droit (aprés avoir travaillé de l'arrière en utilisant un miroir pendant dix ans). J'ai gardé cette tapisserie mais je ne saisis le sens veritable de ce moment que des années après.

Je gardai alors le silence faute de pouvoir partager mon enthousiasme avec les trois seuls tisseurs que je connusse et qui vivaient dans le Nord, a Èdinbourg, à plus de cent soixante kilomètres de chez moi. En fait, il y avait, en Europe et partout dans le monde, de nombreux tisseurs tatonnant de la même manière et se posant les mêmes questions.

Je me sentais coupable parce que je violais "les règles"—règles de la tapisserie qui avaient été discutées en détail pendant mon apprentissage—règles qui n'avaient été établies qu'une dizaine d'années auparavant, aprés avoir enfin vaincu la résistance farouche des ateliers de tapisserie françaises.

WELT TAPISSERIE HEUTE

Ein Vierteljahrhundert kann wenig Bedeutung für ein Verfahren haben, das zwei-sogar dreitausend Jahre in hochentwickelter Form existiert hat.

Heutzutage jedoch, bei dem schnellen Tempo, mit dem sich alle Lebensaspekte ändern und wo in den Kunstkreisen die Tatsache einer Neuerung selbst konsequent gelobt wird, hat auch die Entwicklung der gewebten Tapisserie einen radikalen Umdenkungsprozess durchgemacht.

Mit der Zeit wird sich zeigen, was man als eine bedeutende dauerhafte Entwicklung bezeichnen kann und was nur eine vorübergehende Laune war. Trotz allem fand 1962 die erste bedeutende internationale Tapisserieausstellung statt. Und somit ist es angebracht, ein Vierteljahrhundert später die heutige Tapisserie unter Berücksichtigung der Neuerungen in Betracht zu ziehen.

Ich erinnere mich an einen persönlichen Moment der Entdeckung in 1958, als für mich die Fläche der Tapisserie lebendig wurde. Heute mag diese Entdeckung trivial und alltäglich erscheinen, aber ich erinnere mich an eine grosse stille Erregung—ein verstohlenes Schuldgefühl. Als Lehrling hatte ich verschiedene Materialien, Kettenanscherungen und Proportionen ausprobiert. Beim Weben einer kleinen Tapisserie hatte ich einen Rest von Seinebaumwolle über eine winzige Reihe von gewöhnlichen Wollfäden gewebt. Ich suchte einen bestimmten Weisston, aber es war der Kontrast der Oberfläche zwischen den beiden Materialien, der mich stutzig machte. Innerhalb von einer Stunde hatte ich Reihen mit Leinen, Jute, Rayon, Nähgarn, Seide und verschiedenen handgesponnenen Wollgarnen gewebt. Ich versuchte sogar, Soumakknoten und Noppen aneinander zu reihen. Um in direktem Kontakt mit der sich wandelnden Oberfläche zu bleiben, webte ich von der Vorderseite des aufrechten Webstuhls (nachdem ich jahrelang von hinten mit einem Spiegel gewebt hatte). Ich besitze diese Tapisserie immer noch, aber es hat einige Jahre gedauert bevor mir die tiefere Bedeutung dieser Stunde bewusst wurde.

Ich habe damals geschwiegen, denn ich konnte diese Entdeckung nicht mit den drei anderen Webern teilen, weil sie 100 Meilen nördlich in Edinburgh wohnten. In Wirklichkeit gab es zu der Zeit in Europa und anderen Teilen der Welt viele weber, die ähnliche Entdeckungen gemacht hatten und ähnliche Fragen stellten.

Ich fühlte mich schuldig, weil ich gegen die "Regeln" verstossen hatte—Regeln der Tapisserie, die während meiner Lehrzeit gründlich diskutiert worden sind—Regeln, die endlich nach langem Ringen und Widerstand in den französischen Werkstätten ungefähr zehn Jahre vorher entstanden waren.

I had been taught that a 'proper' weft was an unbleached worsted yarn of a 3/20 count which had been professionally dyed in 3 or 4 shades of some fifteen light fast colours; and that the right warp material was wool. Over a seven year apprenticeship I had spent long months practising hatching techniques, open and closed sheds, slit sewing and linking, mathematically graded curves and shapes, stepping, lines, knotting and all the requirements of 'good' tapestry. We were advised, too, that tapestry was a mural art, essentially flat in design with no perspective, a bias of vertical movements, and ought to have some kind of protective border edge. But really a weaver should be content to follow the full size 'cartoon' drawings. Designing was for artists (in contrast we were also sent to daily drawing classes, given days off to go painting and encouraged to design—all a lively contradiction and an aid to independent thinking).

But there were those other weavers also breaking the rules—even some who never knew these rules, and the first International Biennal, in Lausanne, Switzerland, brought many of these weavers, and their tapestries, together. Wall hangings came from northern and eastern Europe, where the medium had continuous links with handloom weaving. Tapestries came from the established centres in southern and western Europe, from North and South America, and even from Japan. Many of the exhibits were in the 'established' manner, but many, too, were unorthodox, or so it seemed, and it is ironic that Jean Lurçat who had such a major role in earlier establishing the modern French movement, with its precise values and restrictions should also have done so much to bring about the Lausanne event. I have little doubt that if he had been born 25 years later than he was he would have been knotting and tufting with the best; certainly Pierre Pauli, a Lurçat enthusiast, a co-instigator of the Biennal and a wise and tireless worker for tapestry—I can recall devilment in the twinkle of his eyes at this turn of events; this new wave of weavers.

That was in 1962. What were the changes that began then, and what has happened over the ensuing twenty five years?

It is probable that there is a greater area of tapestry woven today than at any other time in history. This is, in part, because the preferred weave is generally much coarser (and therefore faster) than before, and while some of the great centres of tapestry of the past may be less active, there are weavers everywhere, and the process is now established and flourishing in countries and in cultures with little or no previous tapestry tradition.

It is significant too that for the first time in centuries and perhaps for the first time ever there are more women than there are men involved in tapestry at all levels; as designers, administrators, curators, conser-

On m'avait enseigné qu'une trame 'comme il faut' se composait d'un fil de laine peignée de calibre 3/20, spécialement teint dans une quinzaine de couleurs de trois ou quatre nuances chacunes et que la chaine traditionnelle était en laine. Pendant mes sept ans d'apprentissage, je m'étais exercé pendant de longs mois à des techniques de trame: "sheds" ouverts et fermés, fentes cousues et liées, courbes et formes calibrées rigoureusement, noeuds et tout ce qui fait partie de la 'vraie' tapisserie. On nous avait aussi dit que la tapisserie était un art mural, dont le dessin etait essentiellement plat et sans perspective, utilisant de préférence des mouvements verticaux, et qu'elle devrait aussi avoir une bordure quelconque pour la protéger. Mais, en fait, un tisseur devrait se contenter de suivre les cartons grandeur nature. Le dessin était réservé aux artistes (alors qu'on nous faisait suivre des cours de dessin tous les jours et qu'on nous encourageait à peindre et à dessiner pendant nos heures de loisir). Tout cela était en parfaite contradiction et nous poussait à penser pour nous-mêmes.

Il y avait, bien entendu, d'autres tisseurs qui ne suivaient pas les règles. Beaucoup ne les avaient jamais apprises et la premiere Biennale Internationale de Lausanne, en Suisse, mit en contact ces derniers et leurs tapisseries. Les tentures murales provenaient d'Europe du Nord et de l'Est, ou ce moyen d'expression avait établi des liens prolongés avec le tissage fait à la main. Les tapisseries venaient de centres de réputation établie en Europe du Sud et de l'Ouest, de l'Amérique du Nord et du Sud et même du Japon. Un grand nombre de pièces suivait la tradition 'établie' mais il y en avait aussi beaucoup qui en déviaient. Ironiquement, Jean Lurcat, qui avait été en grande partie responsable de l'établissement du mouvement français moderne, régi par des valeurs précises et de nombreuses restrictions, jouait aussi un rôle important dans l'organisation de cette exposition de Lausanne. Je ne doute pas un instant que, s'il était né 25 ans plus tôt, il se serait essayé à toute ces techniques avec les meilleurs. Il en est de même pour Pierre Bauli, admirateur de Lurçat, instigateur comme lui de cette Biennale, travailleur sage et sans relâche dans le domaine de la tapisserie—Si je me souviens bien, ses yeux pétillaient d'enthousiasme devant le tour surprenant que prenait cette exposition: cette nouvelle vague de tisseurs.

C'était en 1962. Quels étaient les changements qui se préparaient alors et que s'est-il passé les vingt-cinq ans qui suivirent?

Il est probable qu'il existe aujourd'hui une plus grande surface tapissée qu'à n'importe quelle autre époque dans l'histoire. En partie, parce que le tissage le plus populaire est en général plus grossier (et donc plus rapide) qu'avant. De plus, bien que certains grands centres de tapisserie du passé soient moins actifs, il y a des tisseurs partout: ce moyen d'expression est maintenant établi et florissant dans des pays et des cultures ayant peu ou pas de traditions dans ce domaine.

Il faut remarquer aussi que, pour la première fois depuis des siècles et peut-être même pour la première fois depuis toujours, il y a plus de femmes que d'hommes qui s'occupent de tapisserie à tous les niveaux: il y a des femmes-artistes, des admin-

Ich hatte gelernt, zum "richtigen" Einschlag ungebleichtes Kammgarn von 3/20 zu verwenden, das in zirka 15 Farben mit 3 oder 4 Abstufungen fachmännisch gefärbt war, und dass das "richtige" Kettenmaterial Wolle sei. Während meiner siebenjährigen Lehrzeit hatte ich monatelang damit zugebracht, mit Schattierungsmethoden zu experimentieren: geschlossene und offene Verknüpfung, Trennen und Verbinden durch Nähen, mathematisch errechnete Kurven und Formen, Linien, Abstufungen, Verknotungen und all die üblichen Dinge der "guten" Tapisserie. Wir wurden auch informiert, dass Tapisserie eine "Wandkunst" sei, also im Grunde flach im Design und ohne Perspektive mit einer Vorliebe für Senkrechtbewegungen, und dass es irgeneine schützende Aussenkontourierung haben müsste. Der Weber sollte in der Tat damit zufrieden sein, den lebensgrossen "Karton"—Zeichnungen zu folgen. Das Entwerfen war für Künstler—im Kontrast dazu nahmen wir täglich an Zeichenkursen teil und wurden zum Malen oder Entwerfen ermutigt—alles war ein grosser Widerspruch und diente als Anregungsmittel zu unabhängigem Denken.

Aber es gab in der Tat andere Weber, die gegen die Regeln verstiessen, sogar einige, die die Regeln nie gekannt hatten. Die erste Internationale Biennale in Lausanne führte viele dieser Weber und ihre Tapisserien zusammen. Die Wandteppiche kamen aus Nord- und Osteuropa, wo das Medium hauptsächlich am Handwebstuhl gearbeitet wurde. Die Tapisserien kamen aus Süd-und Westeuropa, aus Nord-und Südamerika und sogar aus Japan. Viele der Ausstellungsstücke waren nach traditioneller Art angefertigt, viele waren aber auch unorthodox, oder scheinbar so. Es liegt eine gewisse Ironie darin, dass Jean Lurçat sich so sehr um die Ausstellung in Lausanne bemühte, denn er hatte eine grosse Rolle gespielt in der Begründung der französischen Bewegung mit ihrer Präzision und ihren Normen. Ich habe wenig Zweifel, dass er, wäre er 25 Jahre später geboren, mit den Besten geknüpft und experimentiert hätte—zum Beispiel Pierre Pauli, ein Anhänger von Lurçat und ein Mitbegründer der Biennale, der sich in Webkreisen sehr aktiv einsetzt. Ich kann mich an ein Funkeln in seinen Augen erinnern, als er diesen Wendepunkt, diese neue Welle des Webens heranrollen sah.

Das war in 1962. Was geschah? Und welche Stilrichtungen haben sich in den darauffolgenden Jahren durchgesetzt?

Wahrscheinlich werden heutzutage mehr Webarbeiten als je zuvor erzeugt. Es geschieht teilweise durch das bevorzugte gröbere und schnellere Webverfahren. Während einige der grösseren Tapisseriezentren der Vergangenheit weniger aktiv geworden sind, gibt es jetzt überall Weber und die Kunst gedeiht nun in Ländern, die wenig oder keine Tapisserietradition aufweisen können.

Es ist auch von grosser Bedeutung, dass es zum ersten Mal seit Jahrhunderten und vielleicht zum allerersten Mal mehr Frauen als Männer gibt, die mit allen Aspekten der Tapisserie vertraut sind: Designer, Museumsdi-

vators, teachers, writers—and weavers. I risk some wrath (from either or both sexes) but I contend that women have opened up a greater tactile sensitivity and have a greater digital dexterity on the whole, and that is all good. (I recall in the early '50's when it seemed so reasonable that girls were not apprenticed in tapestry 'because after the years of training they would get married, have children and give up weaving'.

There is also irony in the fact that not long ago many people who found employment as tapestry weavers were frequently latent or aspiring painters and artists, but an art education was beyond there reach. Today many weavers come from the ranks of painters, and art students and coming from a creative freedom to a severely controlled and technical discipline is a very different experience from the reverse. The traditional apprenticeship system has diminished. Art schools and frequent workshop classes have taken over much of the teaching and training.

The artist-weaver is now an accepted figure—once unacceptable in many workshops—and where the design process was once precise and pre-determined (although I am convinced that early medieval work gave the weavers a strong interpretive role) this recent period has work woven from the loosest of concepts. At a group workshop level, however, for major tapestry projects and commissions, gallery and museum curators and directors will rather tend to choose or advise that an established (and non-weaving) painter be the designer. This is an entrenched approach, particularly in western European workshops, and was established in the early 16th century when the artist Raphael was commissioned to prepare cartoons for the series 'The Acts of the Apostles'. Yet this approach is uncommon in many other regions where tapestry has long been woven, and less common over the whole history of the medium.

Although early medieval tapestries were influenced by and often originated in the illuminated manuscripts of the period, they soon evolved a language of tapestry and the mannerisms and characteristics grew unselfconsciously out of the weaving process. Coptic tapestry, perhaps the source of medieval tapestry which had flourished earlier in Egypt, had its own particular 'rightness' too, in a unity of process and purpose. Peruvian weaving and, interestingly, the later Norwegian tapestries had no graphic link whatsoever with brush or pen (and this has been a vital characteristic of much post 1960 work.) All these early tapestries were essentially figurative in content. They were largely narrative too, and again in Peru and Norway, were strongly stylised. From the time of Raphael, however, there was a growing and subsequently overwhelming influence from painters and painting and all the movements within this powerful medium. The weaving process became extremely skillful and sophisticated. Anything was pictorially possible and the imitated woven brush stroke was commonplace.

istratrices, des conservatrices, des professeurs, des écrivains—et des tisseuses. Au risque de provoquer l'indignation (de l'un ou des deux sexes), je soutiens que les femmes ont ouvert la voie vers une plus grande sensibilité tactile et qu'elles possédent, dans l'ensemble, une plus grande dextérite digitale. Tout cela est bon: je me souviens que, dans les années 50, on ne voulait pas d'apprenties dans la tapisserie car 'apres des années d'apprentissage, elles se marieraient, auraient des enfants et abandonneraient le tissage'.

Ironiquement, il n'a y pas si longtemps, un grand nombre de tisseurs étaient des aspirants peintres ou artistes qui ne pouvaient s'offrir des cours d'art. Aujourd'hui, il y a beaucoup de tisseurs qui sont sortis des rangs des peintres et des étudiants d'art et évidemment il ne leur est pas facile de passer d'une discipline ou la création est libre à une discipline ou tout est réglementé et très technique. Le système traditionnel d'apprentissage est en voie de disparition. Les écoles d'art et les classes offertes par les ateliers ont presque complètement pris la relève.

Le tisseur-artiste est maintenant accepté alors qu'autrefois il ne l'était pas dans de nombreux ateliers. De même, la tapisserie de ces dernieres années a suivi des concepts relâchés alors qu'autrefois le processus de la conception était precis et déterminé d'avance (bien que je sois convaincu qu'au Moyen-Age les tisseurs avaient une grande liberté d'interpretation). Néanmoins, au niveau du travail d'atelier, certains conservateurs et directeurs de galleries et de musées préfèrent ou conseillent que toute tapisserie importante et toute commission soient d'abord esquissées par un peintre de renom (qui ne sache pas tisser). C'est une conception qui est bien enracinée, surtout dans les ateliers de l'Europe de l'Ouest: elle remonte au debut du seizième siècle, à l'époque où Raphaël avait été chargé de préparer les cartons de la série des 'Actes des Apôtres'. Pourtant cette manière de voir est moins commune dans de nombreuses regions où l'on fait de la tapisserie depuis longtemps et encore moins commune dans l'histoire de ce moyen d'expression.

Quoique les manuscrits illuminés du Moyen-Age aient influencé les premières tapisseries mediévales et qu'ils en soient souvent a l'origine, celles-ci se créèrent rapidement un language propre: le tissage développa inconsciemment ses propres caractéristiques et manierismes. La tapisserie Copte, qui s'était épanouie auparavant en Egypte et qui était peut-être à l'origine de la tapisserie médievale, avait aussi ses "codes" qui lui donnaient une unité de production et d'intention. La tapisserie Péruvienne et, curieusement, les tapisseries Norvégiennes qui se développèrent plus tard, ne se rattachaient absolument pas au dessin ou à la peinture (ceci est une des caractéristiques primordiales des oeuvres qui apparurent aprés les années 6o). Toutes ces tapisseries primitives étaient surtout d'inspiration figurative. Elles racontaient généralement une histoire et celles du Perou et de la Norvège étaient très stylisées. L'influence des peintres, de la peinture et de tous les mouvements qui se développaient à l'intérieur de ce moyen d'expression s'amplifia de plus en plus. La technique du tissage se perfectionna jusqu'à en être très sophistiquée. Tout devint possible pour de nombreux artistes qui reproduirent même les coups de pinceau dans leur tapisserie.

rektoren und -Verwalter, Lehrer, Schriftsteller—und Weber. Ich riskiere, mir den Missmut (von einem oder beiden Geschlechtern) zuzuziehen, wenn ich behaupte, dass Frauen eine grössere taktile Empfindsamkeit und Fingerfertigkeit in die Tapisserie eingeführt haben, und das ist gut so. Ich erinnere mich an den Anfang der fünfziger Jahre, als es so vernünftig schien, dass Mädchen keine Lehrstellen im Weben bekamen, (weil sie nach jahrelanger Lehrzeit sowieso heirateten und Kinder gebährden und das Weben aufgeben würden.

Es ist ironisch, dass vor nicht allzu langer Zeit viele angehende Maler und Künstler Arbeit als Tapisserieweber fanden, aber keine Kunsterziehung bekamen. Es ist schwieriger, von kreativer Freiheit auf ein kontrolliertes und technisches Medium umzusteigen als umgekehrt. Das traditionelle Lehrlingssystem ist am Abklingen. Ein grosser Teil des Trainings und Lehrens ist von Kunstschulen und Werkstätten übernommen worden.

Der Weber wird jetzt als Künstler akzeptiert—wo das Designverfahren einmal präzise und genau geplant war, sieht man in letzter Zeit Webarbeiten, die aus vaguen Ideen entstanden sind. Im Workshopmilieu aber, bei grösseren Projekten und Aufträgen, empfehlen die Museums-und Galleriedirektoren meist einen etablierten (und nicht-webenden) Maler für den Entwurf. Dieses Verhalten ist schon lange üblich, besonders in den westeuropäischen Werkstätten. Es begann Anfang des sechzehnten Jahrhunderts, als Raphael beauftragt wurde, Kartons fur die Serie "Die Handlungen der Apostel" zu zeichnen. Es ist jedoch nicht üblich in Gegenden, wo schon seit langer Zeit gewebt wird.

Obwohl die ersten mittelalterlichen Tapisserien durch die illuminierten Manuskripte entstanden und beeinflusst waren, entwickelte die Tapisserie schon bald ihre eigene Sprache und Besonderheiten, die ganz allmählich durch das Webverfahren entstanden sind. Koptische Tapisserie, vielleicht die Quelle der mittelalterlichen Tapisserie, die vorher in Ägypten ihren Höhepunkt erreichte, hatte auch ihre eigene besondere "Rechtmässigkeit" in Bezug auf Zweckmässigkeit und Verfahren. Die peruanische und später die norwegische Tapisserie war auf keine Weise graphisch durch Pinsel oder Feder beeinflusst (das trifft auch auf Webarbeiten zu, die nach 1960 entstanden sind). All diese ersten Tapisserien hatten im Grunde bildlichen Inhalt. Sie hatten eine erzählerische Qualität und waren in Peru und Norwegen stark stilisiert. Seit Raphaels Zeit gab es jedoch wachsenden und später uberwältigenden Einfluss durch die Malerei und ihre verschiedenen Stilrichtungen. Das Webverfahren wurde immer anspruchsvoller und kultivierter. Bildlich boten sich unzählige Möglichkeiten. Der durch das Weben imitierte Pinselstrich wurde alltäglich.

The late 19th century brought about a further reassessment, this time in England by William Morris and the pre-Raphaelite group. Tapestry was only a part of this influential movement, and although the hangings were heavily overlayed by the Romantic/Heroic style of that time, the underlying treatment had repercussions as far away as in the textiles of Antonin Kybal in Czechoslovakia. The modern French movement under Jean Lurçat has to recognize some roots from Morris, too, with a return to a simple colour range and a prestructured design. Marie Cuttoli's venture in Paris in the '30's, when paintings by Picasso, Braque, Rouault, Dufy and other 'Modern' painters of that period were carried out in tapestry did align tapestry with contemporary paintings but 'the smell of turpentine' was strongly evident in the weaving.

By the '40's and '50's Lurçat's drive and influence had revitalised the French workshops. There was no sign of a painted surface origin in these tapestries. A strong and controlled character surfaced which, when looking back today seems to have links with fabric printings or paper collage—perhaps because of what today would be called insufficient 'hands-on' weaving experience by the Movement's leaders. There were, however, signs of what was to come, particularly in the design work of Marcel Gromaire then Mategot, Prassinos and Tourliere; in the weaving of Denis Dumontet; in the vision of cartonnier Pierre Baudoin and from a short lived but valuable publication "Cahiers de la Tapisserie."

By the early '70's and even from the more orthodox workshops, surface changes and different fibres were being used at least discreetly. Added to colour, tone, shape, line, form, rhythm, scale and imagery this "new" feature was now acceptable. Amongst artist-weavers softer natural and earth colours predominated and the surface grew richer and more heavily tactile. Shaped tapestry (re)appeared: sculptured tapestry; layered tapestry; off-the-wall tapestry—and veritable confection of tufting, knotting, crochet, knitting, applique—all the textile techniques abounded. Everyone, it seemed was into tapestry or had a niece who was. Tapisserie and Patisserie were indeed being confused.

A number of more structured and restrained textile art works, particularly from Japan helped bring about some order. Sensuality yielded to control and this direction reformed under the labels of Art Textiles and Fiber Arts. The medium of tapestry weaving settled down once more—and not without some gains. These changes have left some confusion in Lausanne, and the Tapestry Biennal has to find a new name, or redefine its scope. This, however is surely a healthy outcome from a vital era which the Biennal did so much to foster.

A la fin du dix-neuvième siècle William Morris et le groupe pré-Raphaëlien, apporterent d'autres changements en Angleterre. La tapisserie ne représentait qu'une petite partie de ce mouvement, et bien que les motifs des tentures fussent fortement influencés par le style Romantique/Héroique de l'époque, la technique sous-jacente de fabrication de ces dernières eut des répercussions jusque dans les oeuvres d'Antonin Kybal en Tchécoslovaquie. C'est aussi à cause de Morris, que Jean Lurçat et le mouvement français moderne se mirent à utiliser une palette de couleur plus simple et à suivre à nouveau une esquisse. L'entreprise de Marie Cuttoli à Paris, dans les années 30, à l'époque où on reproduisait sur tapisserie les toiles de Picasso, Braque, Rouault, Dufy et autres Peintres 'Modernes', mit la tapisserie au rang de la peinture contemporaine. Mais 'l'odeur de la térébenthine' se sentait fortement dans le tissage.

Vers les années 40 et 50, l'influence et l'initiative de Lurçat donnèrent une nouvelle vie aux ateliers francais. On ne trouvait plus les traces des surfaces peintes d'avant sur ces tapisseries. Un mouvement puissant et contrôlé se forma: il semble aujourd'hui que ce mouvement était lié au tissu imprimé ou au collage du papier et qu'il était peut-être la conséquence de ce qu'on appelle de nos jours un manque d'experience des chefs du Mouvement au niveau du tissage 'fait-main'. Il y avait par contre des signes avant-coureurs du changement qui se préparait, d'abord dans le travail de conception de Marcel Gromaire, Mategot, Prassinos et Tourlière, puis dans la technique de tissage de Denis Dumontet ainsi que dans la vision du cartonnier Pierre Baudoin et enfin dans l'excellente publication des 'Cahiers de la Tapisserie' qui ne parut cependant que peu de temps.

Vers les annees 70, même les ateliers les plus traditionnels commencèrent à utiliser des fibres différentes et à changer la surface des tapisseries. Ce trait "nouveau" auquel s'ajoutaient couleur, nuance, figure, ligne, forme rythme, échelle et image devint alors acceptable. Les artistes-tisseurs commencèrent à employer de preférence les couleurs tendres et naturelles de la terre et la surface devint plus riche et plus variée au toucher. La tapisserie en relief (re)apparut avec la tapisserie sculptée, la tapisserie en couches et la tapisserie qui ne se pendait plus au mur. Toutes les techniques de tissage foisonnèrent: on se mit à faire des touffes, des noeuds, du crochet, du tricot et de l'appliqué. Tout le monde, semblait-il, faisait de la tapisserie ou du moins avait une nièce qui en faisait. On se mit à confondre Tapisserie et Patisserie.

Certaines oeuvres d'art tissées, d'origine japonaise, avaient conservé une forme plus restreinte et plus structurée et elles contribuèrent à remettre un peu d'ordre. La sensualité laissa la priorité à l'ordre et ce mouvement se regroupa sous les noms d'Art Textiles et d'Art des Fibres. La conception de la tapisserie s'assagit à nouveau—non sans avoir bénéficié de ces changements. Ceux-ci créèrent une certaine confusion à Lausanne et la Biennale de la Tapisserie se voit maintenant dans l'obligation de changer de nom ou de se donner une nouvelle signification. Mais en réalité, ce qui ressortit de la Biennale est très sain et l'exposition de Lausanne contribua largement au développement de la tapisserie dans une ère pleine de vie.

Zum Ende des neunzehnten Jahrhunderts gab es weitere Stilneuerungen—diesmal in England durch William Morris und die Präraphaeliten. Die Tapisserie war aber nur ein Teil dieser einflussreichen Bewegung. Obwohl die gewebten Werke den romantischen Heldenstil der damaligen Zeit darstellten, hatte die den Werken zugrundeliegende Bearbeitung folgenreiche Nachwirkungen, die man sogar in den gewebten Stoffen von Antonin Kybal in Tchechoslowakien sehen konnte. Die moderne französische Bewegung unter der Leitung von Jean Lurcat mit der Rückkehr zu einfachen Farbtönen und geplantem Design hat auch William Morris nachhaltigen Einfluss zu verdanken. Marie Cuttolis Werk der dreissiger Jahre in Paris passte die Tapisserie den Gemälden der damaligen Zeit an, aber der "Geruch von Terpentin" war ganz offensichtlich in den Webarbeiten zu erkennen.

Dies geschah zu einer Zeit, als die Werke von Picasso, Braque, Rouault, Dufy und anderen "modernen" Malern auf das Weben übertragen wurden.

In den vierziger und fünfziger Jahren hatte Lurçats Bestreben und Einfluss die französischen Werkstätten neu belebt. In jenen Tapisserien sah man keine Spur von "bemalten" Oberflächen. Eine starke und kontrollierte Ausdrucksform kam zutage, die im Rückblick an Stoffdrucke oder Papiercollagen erinnert. Es gab jedoch Anzeichen, die auf die Zunkunft hinwiesen, besonders in der Designarbneit von Marcel Gromaire, dann Mategot, Prassinos und Tourliere; in der Webarbeit von Denis Dumontet; in den Ideen des Kartonniers Pierre Baudoin, und in einer kurzlebigen aber wertvollen Veröffentlichung "Cahiers de la Tapisserie".

Am Anfang der siebziger Jahre wurden sogar in den traditionellen Werkstätten wenigstens auf dezente Weise neue Flächengestaltungen und Fasern ausprobiert. Diese Neuerung wurde nun akzeptiert und gehörte zu den anderen Elementen, die beim Weben mitspielen: Farbton, Farbabstufung, Linie, Form, Rhythmus, Massstab und Motiv. Unter Künstlern/Webern herrschten sanfte natürliche Tone und Erdtöne vor und die Oberflächengestaltung wurde abwechslungsreicher und taktiler. "Geformte" Tapisserie tauchte wieder auf: skulpturartige Tapisserie, Schichttapisserie, nicht für die Wand bestimmte Tapisserie—und eine grosse Auswahl an gebauschten, verknüpften, gehäkelten, gestrickten, applizierten Tapisserien. Jeder, so schien es, war an Tapisserie interessiert oder hatte Verwandte, die Tapisseriearbeiten machten. Die Tapisserie wurde in der Tat mit der Patisserie verwechselt.

Eine Reihe von strukturierten und dezenten Textilwerken, hauptsächlich aus Japan, stellte wieder eine gewisse Ordnung her. Die Kontrolliertheit verdrängte die Sinnlichkeit und diese Art der Gestaltung wurde unter der Bezeichnung Kunsttextilien und Faserkunst zusammengefasst. Das Tapisseriemedium beruhigte sich wieder einmal—und nicht ohne Verdienst. Diese Veränderungen hinterliessen ein wenig Verwirrung in Lausanne. Die Tapisseriebiennale muss einen neuen Namen finden oder ihren Rahmen neu definieren. Dieses ist sicherlich ein gutes Resultat einer wichtigen Epoche, die durch die Biennale gefördert wurde.

We have seen the miniature textile movement emerge (more than just a tongue-in-cheek counter to the mural nomad label which the architect Le Corbusier gave to tapestry).

We delighted in the uninhibited work by the Egyptian children from Harrania. (Were they really 'children'—without art influence?)

I have records of tapestries by hundreds of Scots over this 25 years. To my astonishment I have visited some 20 other countries and been enriched by the works of the weavers there. Yet my experience is only a small part of tapestry—and tapestry really is only a minor art form.

There are changes again taking place. The peculiar smouldering nature of richly dyed wool has returned to use. And whilst the weave and the very structure of the work had become the image, figurative illusion has again a place. There has emerged an incongruous affinity between photography and tapestry. And even the ubiquitous hatch reappears.

I have my heroes—and a heroine from my formative years. The names Ron Cruickshank, Pierre Baudoin, Denis Dumontet, Pierre Pauli, Rameses Wissa Wassef, Hannah Reggyn and a lovely old Icelander who couldn't read or write but wove such powerful images—they will probably mean nothing to the young weavers today. Even the heroes and the many heroines of these recent years will slip into the shadows. Copic and Peruvian tapestries may seem less striking, for awhile. The Devonshire Hunting tapestries, the 'Unicorn' tapestries, the 'Apocalypse' at Angers and those still underrated Norwegian works may seem to lose something of their magic. That is as it should be.

This exhibition of Tapestry Today grows from the long past and the recent history of the medium. And reveals glimpses of the works of tomorrow.

Archie Brennan
Maui, Hawaii, January, 1988

On a observé l'épanouissement des miniatures textiles (qui sont beaucoup plus que la contrepartie ironique des tentures nomades comme les appelle l'architecte Le Corbusier).

Nous avons grandement apprecié le travail sans inhibition des enfants Egyptiens d'Arranie. (Etaient-ils vraiment des 'enfants',—libres de toute influence artistique?)

J'ai connaissance de centaines de tapisseries qui ont été tissées par des Ecossais ces 25 dernières années. J'ai visité plus de 20 pays et les travaux des tisseurs locaux m'ont beaucoup appris. Et pourtant, mon expérience se limite à une petite partie de la tapisserie—et la tapisserie elle-même n'est qu'un art mineur.

Il y a à nouveau des changements. On apprecie à nouveau la nature sourde mais spéciale des laines de tons riches. Et, bien que la texture et la structure du travail récréent l'image, l'illusion figurative a retrouvé sa place. La photographie et la tapisserie se sont trouvées des affinités surprenantes. Les ombrages omniprésents ont fait leur réapparition.

J'ai gardé de mes années d'apprentissage mes héros—et mon héroïne. Ils s'appellent Ron Cruickshank, Pierre Baudoin, Denis Dumontet, Pierre Pauli, RamesesWissa Wassef, Hannah Reggyn et un viel Islandais charmant qui ne savait ni lire ni ecrire mais qui tissait des images pleines de puissance. Leur nom n'évoquera probablement aucun souvenir chez les jeunes tisseurs d'aujourd'hui. Meme les héros et les nombreuses héroïnes de ces dernières années se fondront dans l'ombre. Les tapisseries Coptes et Péruviennes impressionneront peut-être moins pendant quelque temps. On pensera peut-être que la tapisserie de 'La Chasse au Devonshire', celles de 'La Licorne' et de 'L'Apocalypse' à Angers et les oeuvres méconnues Norvégiennes n'ont plus la même seduction. Et c'est bien comme cela.

Cette exposition de la Tapisserie d'Aujourd'hui prend racine dans le passé lointain et le passé récent de l'histoire de ce moyen d'expression pour mieux réveler ce que le futur nous apportera.

Archie Brennan
Maui, Hawai, Janvier 1988

Wir haben die Geburt der Miniatur-Textilbewegung miterlebt (das soll mehr als eine Andeutung auf die Bezeichnung sein, die der Architekt Le Corbusier der Tapisserie zuordnete).

Wir waren begeistert von dem spontanen Werk der ägyptischen Kinder von Harrania (waren es wirklich "Kinder"—ohne Kunstausbildung?)

Ich habe in meiner Kartei Information über Hunderte von Werken aus Schottland, Werke, die in diesen 25 Jahren entstanden sind. Ich habe zirka 20 Länder besucht und vieles von den einheimischen Webern lernen können. Meine Erfahrungen sind jedoch nur ein Bruchteil von dem, was sich in der Tapisserie abspielt—und die Tapisserie ist nur eine mindere Kunstform.

Aber es finden auch andere stilistische Neuerungen statt. Die eigentümliche glühende Qualität von gefärbter Wolle wird wieder häufig verwendet. Nachdem das Gewebe und die Struktur des Werkes selbst zum Motiv wurde, hat die bildliche Illusion wieder ihren Platz gefunden. Eine unerwartete Verschwägerung zwischen der Photgraphie und der Tapisserie hat sich herauskristallisiert; sogar die allgegenwärtige Schattierung ist wieder auf der Bildfläche erschienen.

Ich habe meine Helden—und eine Heldin aus meinen ersten Entwicklungsjahren. Folgende Namen haben wahrscheinlich wenig Bedeutung für die jungen Weber von heute: Ron Cruickshank, Pierre Baudoin, Denis Dumontet, Pierre Pauli, Ramesses Wissa Wassef, Hannah Reggyn und ein netter reizender alter Isländer, der weder lesen noch schreiben konnte, aber fesselnde Bilder zu weben verstand. Sogar die Helden und Heldinnen der jüngsten Jahre werden verblassen. Koptische und peruanische Tapisserien mögen eine zeitlang weniger eindrucksvoll erscheinen. Die Devonshire Jagdtapisserien", die "Unicorn" Tapisserien, die "Apokalypse" von Angers und die immer noch unterschätzten norwegischen Werke mögen ein bisschen von ihrem Zauber einbüssen. So soll es wohl sein.

Diese "Tapestry Today" Ausstellung umfasst die langjährige Vergangenheit und die jüngste Geschichte des Mediums. Es verschafft einen flüchtigen Einblick in die Werke der Zukunft.

Archie Brennan
Maui, Hawaii, Januar 1988

ARTISTS

*Invited Artist

*Invited Artist

AUSTRALIAN TAPESTRY TODAY

In Australia today the art of tapestry is still in its infancy compared with European countries which have a solid and rich tradition. And, as with any growing, developing infant it reaches out in many directions with its curiosity, willingness to learn and ability to absorb knowledge and use it in a fresh and vital way.

The late 1960's and early '70's heralded a 'Craft Revival' throughout Australia. Public interest was suddenly stirred to discover and delight in objects made by hand, both past and present, and its growth was encouraged by the setting up of Crafts Councils around the country and small galleries which specialized in showing hand-crafted work. In the wake of this new enlightenment the Victorian Tapestry Workshop was established by the State Government of Victoria in 1976 under the direction of Sue Walker, ostensibly to capitalize on two of this country's best resources—fine painters and fine wool. It became fundamental to the development of the short history of tapestry in Australia.

Our borrowed beginnings stem directly from Edinburgh—Archie Brennan, director of the Dovecot Studios was constant advisor to the process of setting up the Workshop, and his ideas and experience were incorporated into its basic plan. The Edinburgh College of Art, through its Tapestry Department provided an environment in which several Australian weavers spent time exploring their ideas. Some brought this influence back to the Workshop in Victoria, others like Kay Lawrence in South Australia and Rosemary Whitehead in New South Wales developed in a strongly individual way in other States.

The Victorian Tapestry Workshop, in turn, through the committment of its weavers has ensured that the best technical knowledge and the finest qualities of tapestry have been achieved within its walls and have been dispersed without to weavers in the community. Two of its original weavers run weaving courses at Colleges of Advanced Education—Marie Cook at Warrnabool T.A.F. E. College and Merrill Dumbrell at Melbourne College of Textiles. Another, Sara Lindsay, has taught many trainee weavers for the Workshop and run the training programs through which potential weavers have been informed and enabled to excel at their craft. Yet another, Liz Nettleton, has established her own weaving studio specialising in rugs and tapestries, also in Melbourne. Of the artists representing Australia in 'World Tapestry Today', Leonie Bessant, Robyn Mountcastle and Joy Smith are currently working at the Victorian Tapestry Workshop. Although they have developed their own expression in very singular and separate ways they owe the facility of their technique to the demands of being professional weavers.

LA TAPISSERIE AUSTRALIENNE D'AUJOURD'HUI

En Australie, la tapisserie n'en est encore qu'à ses premiers pas comparé à la tradition riche et solide des pays européens. Mais comme chaque enfant qui grandit et se développe, elle se tourne avec curiosite dé tous côtés et se montre capable de tout absorber avant de tout transformer en une matière fraiche et vitale.

A la fin des années 60 et au début des annees 70, il y eut un renouveau des arts artisanaux en Australie. Le public découvrit tout à coup avec grand plaisir des objets du passé ou du présent faits à la main. Des Chambres d'Artisanat s'organisèrent dans tout le pays et encouragèrent l'établissement de petites galleries artisanales. En 1976, à la suite de ce mouvement, le Gouvernement d'Etat de Victoria établit l'Atelier de la Tapisserie de Victoria et en donna la direction à Sue Walker dans l'intention de se servir de deux des ressources les plus importantes du pays—ses excellents peintres et sa laine de première qualité. Ces deux éléments s'avérèrent essentiels au developpement de l'histoire brève de la tapisserie en Australie.

Au début, Archie Brennan, alors le Directeur des Studios Dovecot à Edimbourg nous aida. Ses idées, et ses nombreux conseils furent à la base de l'organisation de notre Atelier. Plusieurs tisseurs australiens se forgèrent des idées nouvelles pendant le séjour qu'ils firent au Collège des Arts d'Edimbourg dans le Département de la Tapisserie. Certains ramenèrent avec eux cette influence à l'Atelier de Victoria, d'autres, comme Kay Lawrence d'Australie du Sud et Rosemary Whitehead de la Nouvelle-Galles du Sud développèrent un style individuel puissant dans d'autres Etats.

Grâce à la dédication de ces quelques artistes, l'Atelier de la Tapisserie de Victoria, a donné à un certain nombre de tisseurs locaux et autres la chance de perfectionner leurs techniques et de fabriquer une tapisserie de première qualité. Deux de ses tisseurs d'origine, Marie Cook du Collége T.A.F.E. de Warrnabool et Merril Dumbrell du College des Arts Textiles de Melbourne, se mirent à donner des cours aux Collèges d'Etudes Avancées. Une autre tisseuse, Sarah Lindsay, a formé de nombreux apprentis pour l'Atelier et a organisé les programmes d'apprentissage qui ont permis à de nombreux débutants d'apprendre et d'exceller dans leur art. Une autre, Liz Nettleton, a ouvert son propre studio et se spécialise en tapis et tapisseries à Melbourne même. Parmi les artistes qui représentent l'Australie dans 'La Tapisserie dans le Monde Aujourd'hui', Leonie Bessant, Robyn Mountcastle et Joy Smith travaillent actuellement à l'Atelier de la Tapisserie de Victoria. Bien qu'elles aient acquis leur style par des voies propres et bien distinctes, elles possèdent toutes trois une grande facilité de technique qui ne vient qu'aux tisseurs (tisseuses) professionnelles.

AUSTRALISCHE TAPISSERIE HEUTE

In Australien steckt die Tapisseriekunst noch in den Kinderschuhen im Vergleich zu traditionsreichen europäischen Ländern. Und, wie jedes heranwachsende Kind in den Entwicklungsjahren wendet es sich in alle Richtungen mit seiner Wissbegierde und Lernbereitschaft und seiner Fähigkeit, Wissen zu verarbeiten und auf eine originelle und lebendige Art anzuwenden.

Ende der sechziger Jahre und Anfang der siebziger Jahre fand in ganz Australien eine Wiederbelebung im Kunstgewerbe statt. Das öffentliche Interesse wurde plötzlich angeregt, handgefertigte Objekte aus der Vergangenheit und Gegenwart zu entdecken und zu schätzen. Das wachsende Interesse wurde verstärkt durch die Gründung von Gewerbeausschüssen und durch kleine Gallerien, die sich darauf spezialisiert hatten, handgefertigte Arbeiten auszustellen. Diese Fortschritte waren der Nährboden für die Gründung des "Victorian Tapestry Workshops" durch den Staat von Victoria in 1976 unter der Leitung von Sue Walker. Auf diese Weise wurde von zwei der besten "Güter" des Landes profitiert—grossartige Maler und erstklassige Wolle.

Die Spuren unserer geborgten Anfänge führen direkt nach Edinburgh—Archie Brennan, der Leiter der Dovecot Studios spielte eine grosse Rolle als Ratgeber—seine Ideen und Erfahrung halfen bei der Planung und Errichtung des Workshops. Die Tapisserieabteilung des "Edinburgh College of Art" stellte einen Arbeitsbereich zur Verfügung, in dem mehrere australische Weber mit ihren Ideen experimentieren konnten. Manche kehrten mit diesen neuen Erfahrungen zum Workshop in Victoria zurück. Andere Künstler wie Kay Lawrence in Südaustralien und Rosemary Whitehead in New South Wales entwickelten ihren eigenen Stil in anderen Staaten.

Durch die Loyalität der Weber im "Victorian Tapestry Workshop" wurde neues Wissen und technische Fähigkeiten in der Webgemeinschaft verbreitet. Zwei der ursprünglichen Weber unterrichten an höheren Ausbildungsstätten—Marie Cook am Warrnabool T.A.F.E. College, und Merril Dunbrell am Melbourner Textiliencollege. Sara Lindsay hat viele Lehrlinge im Workshop unterrichtet und die Trainingsprogramme geleitet, in denen angehende Weber hervorragende Werke vollbrachten. Liz Nettleton hat ihr eigenes Webstudio in Melbourne eröffnet—ihre Spezialitat sind Teppiche und Tapisserien. Die Künstler Leonie Bessant, Robyn Mountcastle und Joy Smith vertreten Australien in der Ausstellung "World Tapestry Today" und arbeiten zur Zeit im "Victorian Tapestry Workshop". Sie alle sind hauptberuflich Weber und haben ihren eigenen Stil auf getrennten Wegen entwickelt.

By its very presence the Workshop makes tapestry accessible to hundreds of people who have never before seen this craft practised—in Victoria it exists as a central core around which the paths of weavers cross and unravel in many directions.

For a country with no tradition in tapestry weaving it is interesting, and perhaps natural that its practitioners have been drawn from other areas of the visual arts—painters and graphic artists in the main. They have consolidated their ideas in areas of the arts or crafts where traditions have been established, and then leapt with inspiration into this discipline which has brought them a new dimension of fulfilment. And they have brought with them, perhaps, a point of view that has not been expressed in woven form before, free of any shackles of the conventional past of weaving and bright with the promise of a future.

Cresside Collette

Cresside Collette is a founding tapestry weaver of the Victorian Tapestry Workshop.

La présence seule de l'Atelier met l'art de la tapisserie à la portée de centaines de personnes qui ne connaissaient rien de cet art avant. L'Atelier devient le centre autour duquel les chemins de nombreux tisseurs se croisent et se dispersent de tous les côtés.

Il est intéressant et sans doute naturel de constater que, dans un pays sans tradition en tapisserie, cela soit les artistes des arts visuels—peintres et dessinateurs—qui soit attirés par ce moyen d'expression. Ils ont d'abord consolidé leurs techniques artistiques et artisanales selon les traditions établies avant de se jeter pleins d'inspiration dans cette discipline qui leur a permis de se donner à fond. Ils apportent peut-être avec eux un point de vue qui n'a jamais été exprimé dans une forme tissée jusqu'à présent: une forme libérée de toutes les entraves du passé conventionnel du tissage et pleine des promesses du futur.

Cresside Collette

Cresside Collette est une tapissiere fondatrice de l'atelier Victorien de la tapisserie.

Der Workshop ermöglicht hunderten von Menschen, das Webverfahren und die Tapisserie selbst aus erster Hand zu begutachten. Der Workshop ist ein zentraler Punkt in Victoria, durch den sich die Wege der Weber kreuzen und in viele Richtungen ausströmen. Es ist interessant und vielleicht ganz natürlich, dass die Weber in einem Land ohne Tapisserietradition aus anderen Bereichen der visuellen Künste, hauptsächlich aus der Malerei und Graphik, angelockt werden. Sie haben ihre Ideen aus traditionellen Gebieten der Kunst und des Gewerbes vereinigt und sind dann mit neuer Inspiration auf diese Disziplin umgestiegen, die ihnen neue Dimensionen des Schaffens eröffnete. Sie haben die Tapisserie mit einer neuen Perspektive bereichert—sie haben sich auf eine originelle Weise in gewebter Form ausgedrückt, frei von den Hindernissen der konventioellen Vergangenheit mit der Hoffnung auf eine strahlende Zukunft.

Cresside Collette

Cresside Collette ist eine der ersten dieses Geschäft gegründet hat. Der name is "Victorian Tapestry Workshop."

Cats on Holiday in Mexico
Chats en Vacances au Mexique
Katzen auf Urlaub in Mexico
42 x 48" 107 x 122cm

Contrast, harmony and simple imagery interest me. With these elements I hope to create balanced drama in my work. It is important to me the day to day weaving is fluid, not dictated by a rigid view of the finished product.

On holiday in Mexico I was amused and appalled by fellow tourists who rushed around temple sites in a few moments, camera glued to their faces, leaving a trail of litter behind them!

Les contrastes, l'harmonie et les images simples m'interessent. Avec l'aide de ces élements, j'espère créer un drame équilibré dans mon travail. Je n'aime pas avoir une idée arrêtée du produit fini et je préfère que le tissage que j'éntreprends chaque jour se fasse d'une manière plus fluide.

Pendant mes vacances au Mexique, je m'amusais et m'epouvantais de voir des touristes comme moi visiter les temples en quelques instants, leur appareil photo collé sur le nez, laissant une traînée de detritus derrière eux.

Ich bin an Kontrast, Harmonie und einfachen Motiven interessiert. Mit diesen Elementen hoffe ich, ausgewogenes Drama in meinen Werken zu gestalten. Es ist wichtig, dass das tägliche Weben fliessend voranschreitet und nicht durch eine versteifte Vorstellung vom vollendeten Werk behindert wird.

Während meines Urlaubs in Mexiko war ich gleichzeitig amusiert und entsetzt über andere Touristen, die in wenigen Minuten mit dem Photoapparat vor der Nase durch die Tempel eilten und eine lange Spur von Abfall hinterliessen!

Leonie
BESSANT
Australia

Untitled
Sans Nom
Ohne Titel
1.5 x 1.5"   4 x 4cm

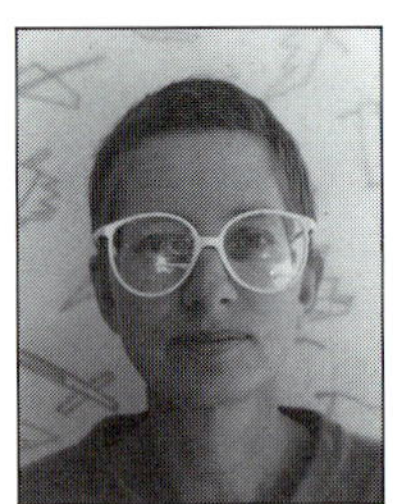

Invited Artist
Lise CRUICKSHANK
Australia

TAPESTRY—as distinct from other methods of weaving—allows freedom in terms of image.
The image is constructed as opposed to applied.
The essence of tapestry is the total integration of construction and image.

Without being bound by tradition—
sensing a link with the past—
adding one thin layer to hundreds of years of tapestry weaving.

LA TAPISSERIE—à l'opposé d'autres méthodes de tissage—
laisse une certaine liberté à l'image.
L'image est construite au lieu d'etre appliquée.
L'essence de la tapisserie est l'intégration totale de la construction et de l'image.

Sans être lié par la tradition—
ressentant un lien avec le passé—
ajoutant une couche mince a des centaines d'années de tissage de tapisserie.

Die Tapisserie—im Gegensatz zu anderen Webarten—ermöglicht mehr Freiheit in Bezug auf das Motiv. Das Motiv wird konstruiert und nicht aufgetragen. Der Kern des Tapisseriewebens ist die totale Integration der Konstruktion mit dem Motiv.

Ungebunden an Tradition-eine Verbindung zur Vergangenheit ahnend-leiste ich einen kleinen Beitrag zum Tapisserieweben, das schon seit Jahrhunderten existiert.

Crossroads, crossed paths, crossing out
Carrefours, chemins de traverse, croisements
Kreuzstrassen, Kreuzwege, Auskreuzen
52 x 59″ 132 x 150cm

I am fascinated by the relationship between drawing and tapestry. All my work begins with drawing, exploring some aspect of my experience. I try not to exert too much control at the beginning, intuitively feeling my way, paring away and refining the idea down to its essentials.

Then, when translating the idea into tapestry the process of exploration begins again . . . how to interpret the subtleties and nuances of paint and pencil into weaving, controlling the richness of the surface, the challenge of working within the formal constraints of the medium . . . all of this makes it an endlessly fascinating, if time consuming process.

Je suis fasciné par la relation entre le dessin et la tapisserie. Tout mon travail commence avec le dessin et l'exploration de certains aspects de mon expérience. Au début, j'évite de prendre une direction trop stricte, préférant suivre mon intuition, épurant mon idée jusqu'à ce que j'arrive à l'essentiel.

Puis, lorsque je transpose cette idée en tapisserie, le travail d'exploration recommence . . . comment transcrire les finesses et les nuances de la peinture et du crayon dans la tapisserie, tout en controllant la richesse de la surface et en restant dans les contraintes formelles de ce moyen d'expression . . . . . . grâce à tout cela, ce processus reste fascinant bien qu'il demande beaucoup de temps.

Ich bin von dem Verhältnis zwischen Zeichnen und Weben fasziniert. Mein ganzes Werk beginnt mit dem Zeichnen und der Erforschung eines Aspektes meiner Erfahrungen. Ich versuche am Anfang nicht zuviel Kontrolle auszuuben, indem ich mich intuitiv vorantaste, die Idee vereinfache und verfeinere, bis das Wesentliche übrig bleibt.

Dann, beim Übertragen der Idee auf das Weben, muss ein neues Problem gelöst werden . . . wie man die Feinheiten und Nuancen von Farbe und Bleistift am Webstuhl interpretiert, wie man die Vielfalt der Oberfläche kontrolliert, wie man den üblichen Anforderungen und Grenzen des Webens gerecht wird . . . all das trifft zusammen in diesem endlos faszinierenden, wenn auch zeitraubenden Medium.

Invited Artist
Kay LAWRENCE
Australia

MICHAEL KLUVANEK

Reaction to Slides
Reactions aux Diapositives
Reaktion auf Dias
70 x 55″   178 x 140cm

Robyn MOUNTCASTLE
Australia

Having always been involved with painting and the graphic arts, I found in recent years, woven tapestry a most responsive and challenging medium. All the skills I may have acquired are called upon.

For me, direct, reactive colour is a strong motivating principle in painting and subsequently tapestry. In "Reaction to Slides" the spontaneous jumble of colour, free of "designed" elements, hopefully stimulates ones subjective response to colour.

Je m'intéresse depuis toujours à la peinture et au dessin. Ces dernières années, je me suis tourné vers la tapisserie car c'est un art qui m'attire et qui est plein de défis. Je peux me servir de toutes les connaissances que j'ai acquises.

Je réagis aux couleurs directes en me mettamt à peindre et bien sûr en me mettamt à tisser. Dans "Réaction aux Diapositives", le tourbillon spontané de couleurs, libre de toute formes dessinées, devrait provoquer chez le spectateur une réponse subjective à la couleur

Ich habe mich schon immer mit der Kunst des Malens und der Graphik beschäftigt. In den letzten Jahren habe ich gewebte Tapisserie als ein sehr zugängliches Medium kennengelernt, das grosse Anforderungen stellt. Ich kann dabei Gebrauch von all meinen erlernten Fähigkeiten machen.

Für mich ist die direkte reaktive Farbe ein starkes motivierendes Prinzip beim Malen und in der Tapisserie. In "Reaction to Slides" (Reaktion auf Dias) hoffe ich, dass der spontane Wirrwarr von Farbe, frei von "entworfenen" Elementen, eine subjektive Reaktion des Betrachters zur Farbe hervorruft.

Parrots, Pirates, & Businessmen
Perroquets, Pirates, & Hommes d'Affaires
Papageien, Piraten und Geschäftsmänner
9 x 8″ 23 x 20cm

London—Brighton train

Dream of parrots and businessmen
Wandering away from the sea
Changing roles.
Pirates, briefcases, pieces of eight,
Umbrellas, sand, stars, bowler hats and patterns.
Getting lost,
Merging into dreams
Coming out, dusted with snowflakes.
Walking carefully over slippery cold
But grey footpaths.
Misty ghosts of spindly trees, old buildings
Full of bright warm surprises—friendly people
Little treasures, pieces of eight.
AArrrr . . . . .

Londres — Le train pour Brighton

Rêves de perroquets et d'hommes d'affaires
S'éloignant de la mer
Changeant de rôles.
Pirates, serviettes, *doublons,*
Parapluies, sable, étoiles, chappeaux melon et dessins.
Se perdre,
Se retrouver dans un rêve
Revenir, couvert de flocons de neige.
Marcher délicatement sur des chemins glissants
Froids et gris.
Fatômes vaporeux de'arbres décharnes, vieux bâtiments
Plein de surpises douces et lumineuses—personnes amies
Petits tresórs, *doublons.*
AArrr . . .

London-Brighton Zug

Traum von Papageien und Geschäftsmännern
Fortwandern von der See
Rollen tauschen.
Piraten, Aktentaschen, Göldstucke,
Schirme, Sand, Sterne, Melonenhüte und Muster.
Sich verlaufen,
In Träume verschmelzen
Erwachen, mit Schneeflocken bestäubt.
Vorsichtig über schlüpfrig kalte aber graue Fusswege gehen.
Nebelhafte Gespenster von spindeligen Bäumen, alte Gebäude
Voller heller, warmer Überraschungen—freundliche Menschen
Kleine Schätze, Goldstücke.
AArrrr . . . . . .

Joy SMITH
Australia

For Jonas
Pour Jonas
Für Jonas
19 x 16″ 48 x 40cm

Rosemary WHITEHEAD
Australia

The process of weaving is essentially boring, but seduced by the medium I am compelled to express my ideas in tapestry. I often feel like Jonah—spewed up on a beach I'd rather not be on. But then there is the inspiring whale, it keeps swallowing me up. Down in its belly I see a magnificent chaos with an underlying structure that provides a rich vitality and wholeness. Maybe it's not so clear down in the belly or on the beach but hopefully the original vision is seen in this tapestry—"For Jonah".

Bein que je trouve le tissage ennuyeux, ce moyen d'expression m'a séduit et j'éprouve le besoin irrésistible d'exprimer mes idées par la tapisserie. Je me compare souvent à Jonas—vomi sur une plage ou je préférerais ne pas être. Mais il y a toujours l'inspiration de la baleine, elle continue à m'avaler. Dans son ventre, je vois u chaos merveilleux sous une structure de base qui donne à l'ensemble une vie riche et unique. Cela ne semble peut-être pas très clair au fond de ce ventre ou sur la plage mais j'espère que la vision premiere se perçoit dans cette tapisserie—"Pour Jonas".

Das Webverfahren ist im Grunde genommen langweilig, aber das Medium verführt mich dazu, meine Ideen in gewebter Form auszudrücken. Ich fühle mich oft wie Jonas—an einem Ufer ausgespuckt, wo ich lieber nicht wäre. Aber dann ist dort der inspirierende Wal, der mich immer wieder verschlingt. In seinem Inneren sehe ich ein phantastisches Chaos, dem eine Struktur von grosser Vitalität und Ganzheit zugrunde liegt. Vielleicht ist es nicht ganz so klar im Inneren oder am Strand, aber hoffentlich kann man die ursprüngliche Idee in dieser Tapisserie erkennen— (Für Jonas).

Survival Tactics
Tactiques de Survie
Überlebungstaktiken
33 x 24″ 84 x 61cm

Tapestry is an exciting and absorbing art form. I have a need to express myself visually, to explore ideas and concepts, colours and shapes and to "create" things. Tapestry satisfies these needs, involving a combination of spontaneity in design and precision in execution.

La tapisserie est une forme d'art passionnante et absorbante. Je ressens le besoin de m'expimer visuellement, d'explorer des idées et des concepts, des couleurs et des formes et de "créer" des choses. La tapisserie satisfait ces besoins car elle combine la spontanéité du dessin et la précision de l'exécution.

Die Tapisserie ist eine reizvolle und fesselnde Kunstform. Ich habe das Bedürfnis, mich bildlich auszudrücken, Ideen, Konzepte, Farben und Formen zu erforschen und Dinge zu "kreieren". Die Tapisserie befriedigt all diese Bedürfnisse durch eine Kombination von Spontanität im Entwurf und Präzision in der Ausführung.

Invited Artist
Kate
WELLS
New Zealand

AMERICAS TAPESTRY TODAY

Far removed from the fast lane of the contemporary art scene, a revolution is taking place, the rebirth of contemporary, woven, flat tapestry. It didn't happen overnight—this "revolution" took five hundred years of evolution. Once the dominant art form of the medieval world, woven tapestry was relegated to second-class "imitator" status during the Renaissance when painting became king. In the late nineteenth and early twentieth century, the fires of this revolution were fanned by flames in two separate countries, the United Kingdom and France. England's William Morris believed that the only way to resurrect woven tapestry was to return to the medieval concepts of excellence. In 1880, at his Merton Abbey Workshops in England, Morris limited his color palette, used medieval techniques for shading and allowed his weavers to interpret the imagery as they saw fit. In 1912, Morris' legacy was carried on at The Edinburgh Tapestry Company (Dovecot Studios) in Scotland. Later, in the 1960's, under Artistic Director Archie Brennan, Dovecot weavers carried Morris' ideas a step further. They worked directly with the artists in tapestry design. To train students, Brennan began a department of tapestry at the Edinburgh College of Art.

In France, painter Jean Lurçat had been experimenting with tapestry designs since 1916. Lurçat studied the "Apocalypse of Angers" the masterpiece of medieval tapestry by Nicholas Bataille's workshop. Like William Morris, Lurçat returned to medieval techniques: limited palette, strong chromatic contrasts, hachures (techniques for shading), simplified design and most important collaboration between weaver and designer. His ideas are still carried out among teachers and students at the Ecole National des Arts Decoratifs in Aubusson, France. In the years that followed, Lurçat took pride in "having spread the tapestry bug all over the world".

These influences from the United Kingdom (William Morris, The Edinburgh Tapestry Company and Archie Brennan) and France (Jean Lurçat) have spread throughout the world to several new generations of weavers.

LA TAPISSERIE AMÉRICAINE D'AUJOURD'HUI

Loin de la scène agitée de l'art contemporain, nous sommes témoins d'une révolution: la tapisserie contemporaine, plane et tissée reprend vie. Cela ne s'est pas produit soudainement—cette "révolution" a mis cinq cents ans. Au Moyen-Age, la tapisserie dominait les arts mais elle fut reléguée au second plan à la Renaissance, se contentant d'imiter la peinture qui était alors en plein essor. A la fin du dix-neuvième et au début du vingtième siècle, les feux de cette révolution furent attisés par deux pays: le Royaume-Uni et la France. En Angleterre, William Morris etait persuadé que le retour au concepts d'excellence du Moyen-Age était le seul moyen de faire revivre la tapisserie. En 1880, dans ses Ateliers anglais de l'Abbaye Merton, Morris se mit à limiter sa palette de couleur, a utiliser les techniques mediévales des ombres et il laissa une certaine liberté d'interprétation à ses tisseurs. En 1912, la Compagnie de Tapisserie d'Edimbourg en Ecosse (les Studios de Dovecot) prirent la suite de Morris. Un peu plus tard, vers les années 60, les tisseurs de Dovecot, menés par le Directeur Artistique Archie Brennan, s'aventurèrent un peu plus loin. Ils se mirent à travailler en collaboration directe avec les artistes qui concevaient et dessinaient les tapisseries. Brennan organisa un département de tapisserie au Collège des Arts d'Edimbourg afin de former des étudiants.

En France, le peintre Jean Lurçat faisait des essais avec des motifs de tapisserie depuis 1916. Lurçat avait étudie "L'Apocalypse d'Angers": ce chef-d'oeuvre de la tapisserie du Moyen-Age était sorti des Ateliers de Nicholas Bataille. Tout comme William Morris, Lurçat reprit certaines techniques mediévales: palette limitée, contrastes chromatiques puissants, hachures (techniques des ombres), dessin simplifié et surtout collaboration entre tisseurs et dessinateurs. De nos jours, les étudiants et les professeurs de l'Ecole Nationale des Arts Décoratifs à Aubusson, en France, suivent encore les traces de Lurçat qui s'enorgueillit d'avoir "contribué à l'expansion de la tapisserie dans le monde".

L'ascendant du Royaume-Uni (avec William Morris, la Compagnie de Tapisserie d'Edimbourg et Archie Brennan) et celui de la France (avec Jean Lurçat) se répandirent à travers le monde et influença toute une nouvelle génération de tisseurs.

AMERIKANISCHES TAPISSERIE HEUTE

Weit entfernt von der schnellebigen aktuellen Kunstszene findet eine Revolution statt: die Wiedergeburt der gewebten, flachen Tapisserie. Dies geschah nicht über Nacht—die Entwicklung dieser Revolution hat 500 Jahre gedauert. Die gewebte Tapisserie, die einst im Mittelalter als dominierende Kunstform vorherrschte, wurde in der Renaissance, als die Malerei König war, als zweitrangige und "imitierende" Kunstform angesehen. Zum Ende des neunzehnten Jahrhunderts und zu Beginn des zwanzigsten Jahrhunderts wurde das Feuer dieser Revolution von zwei verschiedenen Ländern, Grossbritannien und Frankreich, geschürt. Der Engländer William Morris glaubte, dass der einzige Weg zur Wiedergeburt der gewebten Tapisserie eine Rückkehr zum hohen Niveau des Mittelalters erforderte. Im Jahre 1880 beschränkte William Morris in seinen Merton Abbey Workshops seine Farbpalette. Er verwendete mittelalterliche Schattierungsmethoden und gab seinen Webern Freiheit in der Interpretation der Motive. 1912 wurde Morris' Erbe in Schottland bei der Edinburgh Tapestry Company (Dovecot Studios) fortgesetzt. Später, in den sechziger Jahren, führten die Dovecot Weber unter Archie Brennans Leitung die Ideen von Morris noch einen Schritt weiter. Sie arbeiteten direkt mit Künstlern beim Entwurf der Tapisserie zusammen. Zur Ausbildung der Studenten gründete Brennan eine Tapisserieabteilung am Edinburgh College of Art.

In Frankreich hatte der Maler Jean Lurçat schon seit 1916 mit Tapisserieentwürfen experimentiert. Lurcat hatte die "Apocalypse von Angers", das mittelalterliche Meisterwerk aus Nicholas Bartailles Workshop, genau studiert. So wie William Morris verwendete auch Lurçat mittelalterliche Methoden: eine begrenzte Palette, starke chromatische Kontraste, Schattierungsmethoden, vereinfachte Entwürfe; vor allem betonte er die Zusammenarbeit zwischen dem Weber und dem Designer. Seine Ideen bleiben weiterhin bestehen durch die Lehrer und Studenten am École National des Arts Decoratifs in Aubusson, Frankreich. In den folgenden Jahren berichtete Jean Lurçat stolz, "dass er die ganze Welt mit dem Tapisserievirus angesteckt hätte".

Dieser Einfluss aus Grossbritannien (William Morris, die Edinburgh Tapestry Company und Archie Brennan) und aus Frankreich (Jean Lurçat) verbreitete sich unter mehreren neuen Generationen der Weber auf der ganzen Welt.

In North America, their influence was felt only recently. Although there had been several tapestry workshops established in the United States at the turn of the century, public taste was directed toward woven reproductions of period pieces. While these workshops went to great lengths to influence the public toward contemporary tapestry, it wasn't until 1947 that tapestry became recognized as an art form in its own right. The Metropolitan Museum of Art staged an exhibition of the tapestries of Jean Lurçat. It made a lasting impression on several young American painters, among them, Mark Adams and June Wayne who decided to design for the tapestry medium. Because there were no workshops left to execute their designs, these artists had to turn to the talents of European tapestry weavers.

In the 1960's, several significant fiber exhibitions were instituted, among them, the Lausanne Biennale, a biannual exhibition begun as a showcase for tapestry by Jean Lurçat. In North America it was a period of great experimentation. An entire Fiberart movement began, influenced by artists from the Bauhaus, Black Mountain College and the Cranbrook Academy. Individual artists such as Lenore Tawney, Claire Zeisler and Shelia Hicks explored and developed an entirely new language for textile art not in the pictorial element but in the materials itself.

For tapestry, this period loosened the bonds of technique and imagery and opened up areas for experimentation. It attracted a new breed of artist—Canadians Ann Newdigate Mills (who studied tapestry in Scotland and France) and Marcel Marois. Both came from painting backgrounds. Today, these independent artist/weavers infuse powerful, fresh imagery to tapestry. Their independent status allows them the ability to take risks, which gives new vitality to the art form.

The 1970's gave rise to American tapestry workshops. The San Francisco Tapestry Workshop was established as a result of an exhibition of historical tapestries at the De Young Museum. Painter Mark Adams who had studied tapestry design at the hands of Lurçat, was commissioned to design a tapestry which would be woven as an educational exhibit at the museum by weavers trained under the direction of Aubusson tapestry weaver, Jean Pierre Larochette. In the years that followed, Larochette trained many weavers in traditional Aubusson techniques at the Workshop. These beginnings spawned a new generation of independent American tapestry weavers. One of these artists, Ruth Scheuer, established her own gallery and atelier in New York, Scheuer Tapestry Studio.

On ne perçut leur influence que dernièrement aux Etats-Unis. Bien que plusieurs ateliers de tapisserie se soient ouverts aux Etats-Unis au début du siècle, le public s'intéressait surtout aux reproductions des tapisseries des périodes classiques. Malgré tous leurs efforts, ces ateliers n'arrivaient pas à promouvoir la tapisserie contemporaine auprès du public américain. La tapisserie reçut enfin ses lettres de noblesse en 1947. Le Musée Metropolitain d'Art organisa l'exposition des tapisseries de Jean Lurçat. Plusieurs jeunes peintres se montrèrent très impressionnés et Mark Adams et June Wayne, parmi eux, se mirent à dessiner pour la tapisserie. Comme ils ne trouvaient pas d'ateliers pour exécuter leurs projets, ils s'adressèrent à des tisseurs européens.

Il y eut plusieurs expositions des Arts Textiles et Jean Lurçat organisa, en particulier, la Biennale de Lausanne qui se mit a exhiber des tapisseries deux fois par an. L'Amérique du Nord était alors en pleine période expérimentale. Le mouvement de l'Art des Fibres se forma sous l'influence d'artistes venus de Bauhaus, du Collège de "Black Mountain" et de l'Académie de Cranbrook. Certains artistes comme Lenore Tawney, Claire Zeisler et Sheila Hicks se mirent à explorer et à developper un language tout nouveau dans l'art textile: elles changèrent les matériaux tout en respectant les éléments picturaux.

Cette période donna l'occasion à la tapisserie de se libérer de certaines contraintes techniques et picturales et d'ouvrir certaines voies experimentales.

Cela attira de nouveaux artistes comme les canadiens Ann Newdigate Mills (qui a etudié la tapisserie en Ecosse et en France) et Marcel Marois. Tous deux avaient commencé par la peinture. Aujourd'hui, ces artistes/tisseurs indépendants introduisent des images fraiches et puissantes dans la tapisserie. Leur indépendance leur permet de prendre des risques et c'est cela qui donne une vitalité nouvelle à cet art.

Les ateliers américains prirent leur essor dans les années 70. L'Atelier de Tapisserie de San Francisco ouvrit ses portes grace à l'exposition des tapisseries historiques du Musée de De Young. On demanda au peintre Mark Adams, qui avait etudié la tapisserie sous Jean Lurçat, de dessiner une tapisserie. Plusieurs tisseurs, anciens apprentis du tisseur d'Aubusson, Jean-Pierre Larochette, devaient ensuite la tisser devant le public du musée. Larochette enseigna les techniques traditionnelles d'Aubusson à de nombreux tisseurs dans cet atelier. Tout ceci servit de tremplin à une nouvelle génération de tisseurs américains indépendants. Une de ces artistes, Ruth Scheuer, ouvrit sa propre gallerie et atelier à New York, le studio de tapisserie Scheuer.

In Nordamerika spürt man den Einfluss erst seit kurzer Zeit. Obwohl es zur Jahrhundertwende mehrere Tapisserieworkshops in den Vereinigten Staaten gab, verlangte der öffentliche Geschmack gewebte Imitationen von zeitgenössischen Gemälden. Während diese Workshops mit allen Mitteln versuchten, das öffentliche Interesse an Tapisserie zu erwecken, wurde die Tapisserie erst 1947 als autonome Kunstform anerkannt. Das Metropolitan Museum of Art arrangierte eine Ausstellung von Jean Lurçats Tapisserien. Die Ausstellung hinterliess einen tiefen Eindruck bei verschiedenen jungen amerikanischen Malern; unter ihnen, Mark Adams und June Wayne, die sich entschlossen für das Tapisseriemedium zu entwerfen. Diese Künstler mussten sich an europäische Tapisserieweber wenden, da es nun keine Workshops mehr gab, für die sie in ihrem eigenen Land entwerfen konnten.

In den sechziger Jahren gab es mehrere bedeutende Textilausstellungen wie zum Beispiel die Lausanner Biennale, eine jährliche Ausstellung, die als eine Tapisserieshow von Jean Lurçat begann. In Nordamerika war es eine Zeit grosser Experimentation. Eine regelrechte Faserkunstbewegung begann durch den Einfluss vom Bauhaus, Black Mountain College und Cranbrook Academy. Künstler wie Lenore Tawney, Claire Zeisler und Sheila Kicks erforschten und entwickelten eine völlig neue Sprache der Textilkunst in Bezug auf die Materialien.

In der Tapisserie wurde mehr Raum zum Experimentieren geschaffen und eine neue Art von Künstlern angelockt—die Kanadier Ann Newdigate Mills (sie studierte Webkunst in Schottland und Frankreich) und Marcel Marois. Beide hatten eine Ausbildung als Maler durchgemacht. Heute bereichern diese unabhängigen Künstler die Tapisserie durch ihre wirkungsvollen, frischen Motive. Ihr unabhängiger Status gibt ihnen die Möglichkeit, Risiken einzugehen, die der Kunstform eine neue Vitalität verleihen.

In den siebziger Jahren wurden viele amerikanische Werkstätten eröffnet. Der San Franzisko Workshop wurde nach einer Ausstellung von traditionellen Tapisserien im De Young Museum gegründet. Der Maler Mark Adams, der unter Lurcat Tapisserieentwurf studiert hatte, wurde beauftragt, eine Tapisserie zu entwerfen, die für eine Museumsausstellung von Webern unter der Leitung des Aubusson Webers, Jean Pierre Larochette, gewebt werden sollte. In den darauffolgenden Jahren unterrichtete Larochette viele Weber in den traditionellen Aubussonmethoden. Diese Anfänge erzeugten eine neue Generation unabhängiger amerikanischer Tapisserieweber. Die Künstlerin Ruth Scheuer eröffnete ihre eigene Gallerie und besitzt ihr eigenes Atelier in New York "Scheuer Tapestry Studio".

Today, commissioned tapestries hang in public buildings, corporate castles, galleries and homes. North American tapestry is rich from the influences of many cultures, ideas and images. Independent artist/weavers, workshops, schools (Oregon School of Arts & Crafts) and exhibitions (many with government support) are pursuing and promoting the rebirth of an art form. Forums, such as the American Tapestry Alliance are providing a free interchange of ideas. Today, North American tapestry is alive, well and thriving. As in any revolution, new ideas are introduced and only the best traditions retained.

Valerie Clausen

Valerie Clausen is a freelance writer and curator of the exhibition "Tapestry: Contemporary Imagery / Ancient Tradition United States, Canada, United Kingdom".

Aujourd'hui, il a des tapisseries de commande sur les murs des batiments publics, des chateaux appartenant à certaines corporations, des galleries et des maisons particulières. La tapisserie de l'Amérique du Nord est particulièrement riche car elle est influencée par de nombreuses cultures, idées et images. Les artistes/tisseurs indépendants, les ateliers, les écoles (L'Ecole des Arts et de L'Artisanat d'Oregon) et les expositions (souvent financièrement soutenues par le gouvernement) protègent et encouragent la renaissance de cet art. Des forums, comme celui de l'Alliance Americaine de la Tapisserie permettent un échange libre des idées. Aujourd'hui, la tapisserie de l'Amérique du Nord est en plein essor. Comme dams toute révolution, il n'y a que les meilleures traditions parmi les idées nouvelles qui restent.

Valerie Clausen

Valerie Clausen écrit des articles. Elle est aussi la conservatrice de l'exposition "Tapisserie Contemporaine et Images Traditionnelles: Etats-Unis, Canada, Royaume-Uni"

Heute gibt es Tapisserien in öffentlichen Gebäuden, Schlössern, Gallerien und Privatheimen. Die nordamerikanische Tapisserie wird durch verschiedene Völker, Ideen und Motive inspiriert. Unabhängige Künstler, Weber, Workshops, Schulen (Oregon School of Arts and Crafts) und Ausstellungen (viele mit staatlicher Hilfe) unterstützen und fördern die Wiedergeburt einer Kunstform. Vereine wie die "American Tapestry Alliance" ermöglichen einen freien Ideenaustausch. Heute gedeiht die nordamerikanische Tapisserie und steckt voller Leben. Wie bei jeder Revolution, tauchen neue Ideen auf, die nur mit den besten Traditionen verknüpft werden.

Valerie Clausen

Valerie Clausen ist eine freiberufliche Schriftstellerin und die Ausstellungsleiterin für "Tapestry Contemporary Imagery Ancient Tradition United States, Canada, United Kingdom".

GUY COUTURE

After You
Apres vous
Nach Ihnen
56 x 43″ 142 x 109cm

Sometimes in my mind, I catch a glimpse of surprising images that I feel I must urgently materialize. Then I start drawing and drawing, and in front of my eyes heads, human figures and animals appear, a whole world of vibrating colours. Through them is often expressed a satirical and humoristic vision of reality, but, at a deeper level, a quest for serenity and plenitude. Out of those images will come a tapestry, which will allow me to give them a specific softness, brightness, richness and depth.

Quelquefois, j'entrevois dans ma tête des images étonnantes, qu'il devient urgent pour moi de matérialiser. Alors je dessine, je dessine, et devant mes yeux apparaissent des têtes, des personnages, des animaux, tout un monde vibrant de couleurs. A travers eux s'exprime souvent une vision satirique et humoristique des choses, mais aussi, plus profondément, une quête de sérenité et de plénitude. De ces images naîtra la tapisserie, qui me permettra de leur donner un velouté, un brillant, une richesse et une profondeur particulière.

Manchmal kommen mir erstaunliche Bilder in den Sinn, die ich unbedingt in materielle Form umsetzen muss. Dann beginne ich zu zeichnen und vor meinen Augen erscheinen Gesichter, menschliche Figuren und Tiere—eine ganze Welt voller vibrierender Farben. Durch sie wird oft eine satirische und humoristische Version der Realität ausgedrückt, aber auf einer tieferen Ebene ist es ein Streben nach Ruhe und Vollkommenheit. Es entsteht eine Tapisserie mit Motiven, die eine gewisse Sanftheit, Klarheit, Fülle und Tiefe haben.

Elène
GAMACHE
Canada

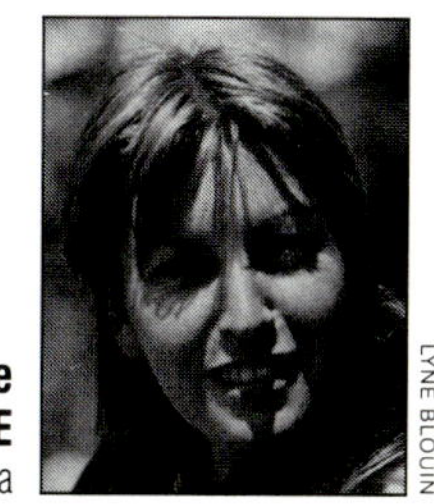

LYNE BLOUIN

JOHN DEAN

African Skies
Ciels Africains
Afrikanischer Himmel
56 x 54"   142 x 137cm

Murray GIBSON
Canada

I am currently exploring the spiritual relationship that exists between isolated cultures and their environment. These societies have an instinctual reaction to Nature and have created myths and legends that define their existence in this world. They worship gods who personify the natural forces that set the rhythm of their lives.

The patterns I use come from two sources. The first is from the primitive cultures themselves—I am inspired by the motifs that decorate their tools,

Je suis en train d'explorer les relations spirituelles qui existent entre les cultures isolées et leur environnement. Ces sociétés ont une réaction instinctive face à la Nature et elles ont créé des mythes et des légendes qui définissent leur existence dans le monde. Elles adorent les dieux qui personnifient les forces naturelles qui donnent le rythme à leur vie.

Les motifs que je choisis proviennent de deux sources. Je me sers d'abord des cultures primitives elles-mêmes—je m'inspire des motifs qui ornemen-

Ich erforsche gerade die geistige Beziehung zwischen isolierten Völkern und deren Umgebung. Diese Völker reagieren instinktiv auf die Natur. Sie erfinden Mythen und Legenden, um ihrer Existenz auf dieser Welt Sinn zu geben. Sie verehren Götter, die natürliche Mächte personifizieren, welche wiederum den Rhythmus ihres Lebens bestimmen.

Die Muster, die ich verwende, stammen aus zwei Bezugsquellen. Die erste Quelle sind die primitiven Völker selbst—ich finde Inspiration in den Motiven,

(▶ 75)

D. JAMES DEE

Zeus lies in Ceres' bosom
Zeus sur le sein de Ceres
Zeus liegt an der Brust von Ceres
48 x 60″ 122 x 153cm

I awake and with paint I find the image. It needs more substance. With weaving I build it again, from thousands of little hand motions. The image is upside down and backwards on the loom. I learn to see with my hands, and to dream with my eyes wide open.

Je me réveille et avec la peinture je trouve l'image. Elle a besoin de plus de substance. En tissant je la recontruis à l'aide de mille petits mouvements de la main. L'image est à l'envers sur le métier à tisser. J'apprends à voir avec mes mains et à rêver les yeux grands ouverts.

Ich erwache und finde das Motiv durch die Farbe. Es braucht mehr Substanz. Beim Weben konstruire ich es auf's Neue mit Tausenden von kleinen Handbewegungen. Das Motiv steht auf dem Kopf und hängt umgekehrt am Webstuhl. Ich lerne, mit meinen Händen zu sehen und mit offenen Augen zu träumen.

Ruth JONES
Canada

Interception between the Visible and the Invisible
Interception entre le visible et l'invisible
Absperrung zwischen dem Sichtbaren und dem Unsichtbaren
32 x 78" 81 x 198cm

J. RENÉ ARCHAMBAULT

Invited Artist
Marcel MAROIS
Canada

Why do I believe it is so important to create in the field of tapestry? I've always had difficulties answering that type of question.

I started taking tapestry classes in 1969, at a time that still valued the classical tapestry through the medium of Michel Tourliere, Mario Prassinos and Robert Wogensky's works whose contemporary mural language revived tapestry through the symbolism of the image and the expression of colour. At the same time the expressionism of Magdalena

Pourquoi est-ce que j'accorde autant d'importance à créer dans le domaine de la tapisserie? J'ai toujours eu beaucoup de difficultés à répondre à ce type de questions.

J'ai commencé à suivre des cours de tapisserie en 1969, période qui valorisait encore la tapisserie classique par l'intermédiaire des oeuvres de Michel Tournalière, Mario Prassinos et Robert Wogensky dont le langage mural contemporain renouvelait la tapisserie par la symbolique de l'image et l'expres-

Warum ist es mir so wichtig, auf dem Gebiet der Tapisserie kreativ tätig zu sein? Es ist mir schon immer schwergefallen, diese Frage zu beantworten.

Ich begann 1969, an Tapisseriekursen teilzunehmen. Das war zu einer Zeit, in der man in der klassischen Tapisserie noch den Einfluss von Michel Tourliere und Mario Prassinos spürte. Auch schätzte man damals Robert Wogenskys Werk, dessen zeitgemässe Wandteppiche die Tapisserie durch Symbolismus und farblichen Ausdruck wiederbelebten. Zu

(▶ 76)

GRANT KERNAN

Looking for a good ancestor
A la Recherche d'un Bon Ancetre
Auf der Suche nach einem guten Vorfahren
33 x 51"   84 x 130cm

The tapestry medium is important to me — because it is as important as fresh air, clean rivers, uncontaminated fruit, healthy babies and endangered species of animals.

But on the other hand it is also important that we resist the nostalgia that is associated with the medium. Idealizing an old social order carries the danger of closing ones eyes to vital issues which are a threat to the good things in life — such as tapestry.

A mon avis, la tapisserie a autant d'importance que l'air frais, les rivières sans pollution, les fruits sains, les enfants en bonne santé et les animaux en voie de disparition.

Mais d'autre part, il faut aussi éviter de se laisser influencer par la nostalgie qui est associée à ce moyen d'expression. Lorsqu'on idéalise un ordre social ancien, on court le risque de laisser de côté des questions vitales qui preséntent un danger pour

Das Tapisseriemedium ist für mich bedeutend, weil es genauso wichtig ist wie frische Luft, unverseuchte Flüsse, unbespritztes Obst, gesunde Babies und gefährdete Tierarten. Aber auf der anderen Seite ist es mir wichtig, dass wir uns der Nostalgie, die mit dem Medium verknüpft ist, widersetzen. Es besteht eine Gafahr darin, eine alte Ordnung zu idealisieren und grundlegende Punkte zu ignorieren, die die guten Dinge im Leben, wie zum Beispiel Tapisserie, bedrohen.

(▶ 77)

Invited Artist
Ann Newdigate MILLS
Canada

JOSEPHINE MILLS

Lukas II
39 x 55" 99 x 140cm

FRANK ENGEL

Cecilia BLOMBERG
U.S.A.

For years I have had this picture of Lukas, who owns a simple restaurant on a beach in Cyprus. The memory of finding this friend who introduced us to his island was so strong it had to become a tapestry.

To me weaving is an art form beyond painting, with more richness in color and texture and full of challenges.

Cela fait des années que j'ai cette photographie de Lukas qui est le propriétaire d'un petit restaurant sur une plage de Chypre. Sa rencontre et notre introduction à l'île de Chypre avaient laissé un souvenir tel que je les avais transposés dans cette tapisserie.

A mon avis, le tissage est un art qui va plus loin que la peinture, qui est plus riche en couleur, en texture et qui est plein de défis.

Seit Jahren habe ich deses Bild von Lukas, der ein einfaches Restaurant am Strand von Zypern besitzt. Die Erinnerung an diesen Freund, der uns mit seiner Insel bekanntmachte, war so stark, dass daraus eine Tapisserie entstehen musste.

Für mich ist das weben eine Kunstform, die über das Malen hinausgeht durch grösseren farblichen sowie strukturellen Gehalt und es stackt voller Probleme, die es su lösen gibt.

BRUCE HANDELSMAN

Untitled Abstract
Abstrait Sans Nom
Abstrakt ohne Titel
55 x 39″ 140 x 99cm

In collaboration with watercolorist BONNIE BOREN

Whether my idea for a tapestry begins with a thought, a watercolor, or photographs, I want the concept itself to remain unchanged. Before weaving, I turn my composition into a line drawing, and choose my wool palette. For me, the enjoyment and creativity happen on the loom. I choose colors and techniques as I weave. I don't think of my weaving as an interpretation of the design, but as the actual creation, with the original idea in mind. As a collaboration, this piece grew through both our efforts and continued to evolve on the loom.

Quelle que soit la source de mon inspiration, une pensée, une aquarelle ou une photographie, je ne change rien à la conception même de ma tapisserie. Je dessine ma composition et je choisis ma palette de laine. Le travail sur le métier à tisser éveille mon plaisir et mon esprit de création. Je décide des couleurs et des techniques en tissant. Mon travail de tissage n'est pas l'interprétation du dessin mais la création véritable de l'idée originale que j'ai en tête. Ainsi cette tapisserie, qui est le résultat de notre collaboration, est née petit à petit sur le métier à tisser.

Ich möchte, dass die Idee fur die Tapisserie unverändert bleibt, egal, ob sie mit einen Gedanken, einem Aquarell, oder mit Photos beginnt. Bevor ich mit dem Weben beginne, zeichne ich die Komposition und wähle dann meine Wollpalette. Fur mich beginnt der Spass und die Kreativitat am Webstuhl. Ich wahle die Farben und Methoden während ich webe. Ich empfinde mein Weben nicht als eine Interpretation des Entwurfs, sondern als die eigentliche Kreation selbst mit dem Gedanken an die ursprüngliche Idee. Dieses Werk entstand als Zusammenarbeit und entwichelte sich am Webstuhl weiter.

Tricia GOLDBERG
U.S.A.

ALBERT MARSHALL

Aria
Arie
36 x 54"   91 x 137cm

David
JOHNSON
U.S.A.

I began studying piano at age seven and have a deep love for the beauty and discipline of the classical repertoire. I did not begin weaving until I was thirty, so, in a sense, I have come to the art of weaving through music.

The rhythmic processes of weaving seem analogous to music, and as my work progresses I am concerned more and more with making music the product of weaving as well. I use calligraphic motives and figurative forms to represent melodic and rhythmic elements. Harmonic structure and tonal color are related to yarn colors and shading.

J'ai commence à étudier le piano à l'âge de sept ans et je ressens un amour profond pour la beauté et la discipline du repertoire classique. J'avais déjà trente ans quand je me suis mis à tisser et en quelque sorte, je suis venu à la tapisserie grâce à la musique.

Le procedé rythmique du travail de tissage ressemble à la musique et j'essaie petit à petit de tranformer ma création tissée en composition musicale. Je me sers de caractères caligraphiques et de formes figuratives pour représenter des éléments rythmiques et mélodiques. La structure harmonique et la tonalité des teintes sont liées aux couleurs et aux nuances des écheveaux.

Ich lernte Klavierspielen, als ich sieben Jahre alt war. Ich empfinde eine tiefe Liebe fur die Schönheit und Disziplin des klassischen Repertoires. Erst als ich ungefähr dreissig war, begann ich zu weben. Also, gewissermassen hat mich die Musik zur Webkunst geführt.

Der rhythmische Verlauf des Wbens erinnert mich an Musik. Je weiter ich in meiner Arbreit fortfahre, desto mehr bin ich daran interessiert, auch die Musik ein Product des Webens zu machen. Ich verwende Kalligraphische Zeichen und bildliche Formen, um melodische und rhythmische Elemente zu vermiteln. Die Tonalitat und die harmonische Struktur sind mit den Farben und Schattierunger des Garns verwandt.

Sea Breeze
Brise Maritime
Meeresbrise
48 x 73" 122 x 186cm

My interest in tapestry weaving began when I learned enough about traditional techniques of Aubusson tapestry to discover its uncanny potential for giving life to illusional images of fabric elements and to suspend this moment in time. I am concerned that the main impact of the work on the viewer be the sense of mystery, fantasy and confrontation evoked by the interaction of free-floating fabric interacting with a space defined by a somewhat unlikely architectural and atmospheric environment, enlivened by pattern and color. The reaction to the image should be concurrent with the realization that the work is rendered in fabric and that the content of the work and the material in which it is rendered are so interdependent that one cannot easily exist without the other.

J'ai commencé à m'intéresser à la tapisserie après avoir bien appris les techniques de la tapisserie d'Aubusson. J'ai découvert alors qu'elle avait le pouvoir merveilleux de donner la vie à des images illusoires faites à partir d'étoffes et de suspendre cet instant dans le temps. Je veux surtout que mon travail provoque chez celui qui le regarde une impression de mystère, de fantaisie et de confrontation; impression suscitée par l'intéraction de morceaux d'étoffes flottants dans un espace limité par un environnement et une structure tant soit peu surprenante à qui la forme et la couleur donnent vie. Confronté à l'image, le spectateur devrait immédiatement réaliser qu'elle est reproduite avec du tissu et que le contenu et la matière dont elle est faite sont si étroitement liés qu'il devient difficile à l'un d'exister sans l'autre.

Mein Interesse am Tapisserieweben begann, als ich durch die traditionellen Methoden der Aubusson Tapisserie das ungeheure Potential erkannte, illusionären Motiven aus Stoffelementen Leben zu verleihen und den Moment in der Zeit festzuhalten. Es ist mir wichtig, dass der Haupteindruck des Betrachters einen Hauch von Rätsel, Phantasie und Konfrontation in sich trägt. Dieser Eindruck soll durch die Spannung entstehen, die sich aus dem Spiel der freischwebenden gewebten Formen innerhalb des architektonischen und atmosphärischen Raumes ergibt,der durch Muster und Farbe belebt wird. Bei der Reaktion auf das Motiv sollte man bedenken, dass das Werk in Stoff gearbeitet ist und dass der Inhalt des Werkes und das Material so voneinander abhängig sind, dass das Eine ohne das Andere nicht ohne weiteres existieren kann.

Ann
KEISTER
U.S.A.

MARK SCHWARTZ

Light Rain
Pluie Legere
Leichter Regen
62 x 53″ 158 x 135cm

Invited Artist

Jean Pierre & Yael Lurie
LAROCHETTE

U.S.A.

Expressing that which belongs to the language of an established tradition—by communicating something that can not be rendered in any other way—the making of tapestries today is no different then it was generations ago. And yet, in each new work we find that uniqueness, that mapping of a discovery unraveling in the familiar task of weaving.

Although tapestry requires a relatively simple technique, a basic "fabrication", its design possibilities are limitless. As the work goes, weaving after weaving, skills growing by repetition, we get to know the process a little further and still wonder persists.

La création de tapisseries aujourd'hui n'est pas différente de celle des générations passées: elle exprime ce qui appartient au language d'une tradition établie en communiquant quelque chose qui ne peut être transmis d'aucune autre manière. Et pourtant, dans chaque oeuvre nouvelle nous trouvons quelque chose d'unique et qui se révèle dans la tache familière du tissage. Quoique la tapisserie ne requiert qu'une technique relativement facile, une simple "fabrication", ses possibilités de création sont illimitées. Notre adresse de tisseur s'améliore à force de répétition, nous apprenons de plus et pourtant notre admiration persiste.

Das Weben von Tapisserien ist heutzutage nicht anders als vor etlichen Generationen—es drückt die Sprache einer seit langem bestehenden Tradition aus, indem es etwas vermittelt, was auf keine andere Weise wiedergegeben werden kann. Und trotzdem findet man in jedem neuen Werk dieses Einzigartige, diese Spuren einer Entdeckung, die wahrend der gewohnten Beschäftigung des Webens zutage kommen.

Obwohl in der Tapisserie eine relativ einfache Methode verwendet wird, im Grunde ein rein "technisches Verfahren", sind die Designmöglichkeiten unbegrenzt. Je weiter sich das Werk nach langem Weben entwickelt, je grössere Fortschritte die Fähigkeiten durch unzählige Wiederholung machen, desto besser lernt man das Verfahren kennen—aber fasziniert ist man immer noch.

Secret Garden
Jardin Secret
Geheimer Garten
47 x 69"   120 x 175cm

My work is currently concerned with expressing the concept of *genius loci* or "spirit of place". Early writers and philosophers felt that 'there was a difference between the atmosphere surrounding one place and another . . . that a locality might possess a spirit of its own'. The recognition of, and fascination with, this phenomenon has been the conceptual basis of my tapestries since 1983.

"Secret Garden" is one of a series of pieces concerning the garden. Here I am interested in presenting the garden as the kind of secret place where one's dreams and imagination run wild.

Dans mon travail, je cherche à exprimer l'idée de *genius loci* ou "esprit d'un lieu". Les premiers écrivains et philosophes croyaient "qu'il avait une différence entre l'atmosphère qui émamait de lieux divers . . . que chaque endroit possédait un esprit qui lui était propre". La reconnaissance et la fascination de ce phénomene est à la base de mes créations depuis 1983.

"Jardin Secret" appartient à la série des oeuvres centrées autour du thème du jardin. J'essaie d'y présenter le jardin comme un endroit secrêt ou les rêves et l'imagination de chacun peuvent vagabonder en toute liberté.

In meiner Arbeit befasse ich mich zur Zeit mit dem Konzept des genius loci oder "Seele des Ortes". Die alten Schriftsteller und Philosophen spürten, dass "es einen Unterschied zwischen der Atmosphäre eines Ortes und der Atmosphäre eines anderen Ortes gibt . . . dass dieser Ort selbst eine eigene Seele besitzt". Diese Erkenntnis und die Faszination mit diesem Phänomen ist seit 1983 die konzeptive Basis meiner Tapisserien.

"Secret Garden" (heimlicher Garten) ist ein Werk in einer Serie über diesen Garten. Hier bin ich daran interessiert, den Garten als eine Art geheimen Ort darzustellen, in dem man seinen Träumen und seiner Phantasie freien Lauf lassen kann.

Sharon
MARCUS
U.S.A.

AARON JOHANSON

SHELDON HELFMAN

Liberation—*We salute our liberators*
Liberation—*Nous Saluons Nos Liberateurs*
Befreiung—*Wir grussen unsere Befreier*
36 x 47" 91 x 119cm

T V VESSELL

Muriel NEZHNIE
U.S.A.

During twenty-nine years of custom design tapestry work I have also produced personal tapestries incorporating human imagery and social content. I chose handwoven tapestry because it is a beautiful and enduring medium of expression. Its natural materials, usually wool, cotton or silk, are pliable and sensuous as they accrue by increments beneath one's fingers. Woven forms and images appear from a structuring process that has a unique integrity; a physical and tactile substance unlike a painting, photograph or sculpture. I have found no better or more satisfying vehicle for my work.

Durant les vingt-neuf années ou j'ai fait de la tapisserie sur commande, j'ai également produit de la tapisserie personnelle incorporant des images humaines et un contenu social. J'ai choisi la tapisserie faite à la main parce que c'est un moyen d'expression à la fois beau et durable. Les matériaux naturels qui y sont utilisés, généralement la laine, le coton ou la soie, sont souples et sensuels au toucher tandis qu'ils s'accumulent par couches successives sous les doigts. Les formes et les images tissées naissent d'un processus de structure dont l'intégrité est unique; une substance physique et tactile apparait, différente d'une peinture, d'une photographie, ou d'une sculpture. Je n'ai pas trouvé de moyen d'expression meilleur ou plus satisfaisant pour mes oeuvres.

In den 29 Jahren meiner Webarbeiten für bestimmte Kunden habe ich auch persönliche Wandteppiche mit menschlichen Motiven und sozialer Thematik entworfen. Ich habe handgewebte Tapisserie gewählt, weil sie ein dauerhaftes und schones Ausdrucksmedium ist. Das natürliche Material—meist Wolle, Baumwolle oder Seide—ist so geschmeidig und sinnlich wie es Schritt für Schritt unter den Händen zur Form wird. Gewebte Formen und Motive entstehen durch einen strukturellen Vorgang von einzigartigem Charakter; von physischer und fühlbarer Substanz, ganz anders als ein Gemälde, eine Photographie oder eine Skulptur. Ich habe bisher kein besseres oder befriedigenderes Ausdrucksmittel für meine Arbeit gefunden.

The Imperials
Les Imperiaux
Die Kaiser
75 x 38″ 190 x 97cm

Earlier on, having studied painting, drawing, print making, and ceramics gave a basis for entry into tapestry—which was accidental, really.

But all the above training surely can help prepare one for tapestry designing and weaving.

J'avais d'abord etudié la peinture, le dessin, la gravure et la céramique, ce qui m'avait donné une bonne base avant de me mettre, tout à fait par hasard, à la tapisserie.

Cette éducation prépare sans aucun doute à la conception et au tissage de la tapisserie.

Mein früheres Studium im Malen, Zeichnen, in der Graphik und der Keramik war die Basis meiner Einführung in die Tapisserie . . . das geschah eigentlich ganz zufällig.

Meine Ausbildung war eine grosse Hilfe, indem sie mich gut auf das Tapisserieentwerfen und -weben vorbereitete.

(▶ 77)

Invited Artist
Hal PAINTER
U.S.A.

BEVERLY GODFREY, weaver

The Messenger
Le Messager
Der Bote
42 x 60″ 107 x 153cm

Invited Artist
Ruth SCHEUER
U.S.A.

"THE MESSENGER" is one of a series of tapestries on the subject of how people coexist in crowded areas in the urban environment. Tapestry is used to convey the layers of transparent reflections in glass, a metaphor for the mental walls that an urban person must surround himself with in order to be able to act freely in very crowded situations. Strangers meet, overlap, and touch each others lives without leaving any visible imprint. The viewer is aware of the figure as it is transposed by the constantly changing reflections in the glass, the shadows and patterns of our perceptions.

LE MESSAGER fait partie de la serie des tapisseries qui se groupent autour du thème de la coexistence des hommes dans les quartiers urbains surpeuplés. La tapisserie est le véhicule qui permet de montrer les reflets transparents successifs dans le verre, métaphore des murs mentaux dont l'humamité urbaine doit s'entourer pour garder sa liberté d'action dans les milieux surpeuplés. Des étrangers se rencontrent, se fondent, s'effleurent sans laisser d'empreintes visibles. Ce sont les reflets des ombres et des formes que nous percevons et qui changent constamment dans le verre qui communiquent ce concept au spectateur.

"The Messenger" (der Bote) ist eine Tapisserie in einer Serie über das Zusammenleben von Menschen in gedrängten Stadtgegenden. Ich benutze die Tapisserie zur Darstellung der transparenten Reflektionen im Glas—das ist eine Metapher für die inneren Mauern, die ein Stadtmensch braucht, um sich in beengten Situationen frei bewegen zu können. Fremde treffen sich, überschneiden sich, und berühren das Leben Anderer ohne sichtbare Spuren zu hinterlassen. Der Betrachter ist sich der Figur bewusst, wie sie mit dem beständigen Wechsel der Reflektionen im Glas durch die Schatten und Formen unserer Wahrnehmungen gleitet.

JANICE FELGAR

Duality
Dualite
Dualität
35 x 46" 89 x 117cm

As a fiber artist I have concentrated on tapestries, handwoven in the traditional manner, but contemporary in imagery, design and use of color.

Much of my work explores the theme of duality, the dynamic interaction between interdependent opposites, and the resultant mysteries and ambiguities, conflicts and complements arising from the adversarial relationship of these opposites. Duality is often expressed symbolically by the oriental symbol of yin and yang, and metaphorically by the

En tant qu'artiste en fibres, je fais surtout des tapisseries tissées à la main de forme traditionnelle tout en utilisant des motifs, des dessins et des couleurs contemporains.

Presque tout mon travail explore le thème de la dualité, de l'intéraction dynamique entre deux opposés interdépendants ainsi que les mystères, ambiguités, conflits et éléments complementaires qui sont le résultat de la rélation adverse de ces opposés. Souvent, le symbole oriental du yin et du

Als Webkünstlerin habe ich mich auf traditionelle handgewebte Wandteppische spezialisiert, die aber vom Motiv, vom Design und von der Farbe her zeitgemäss sind.

In vielen meiner Werke erforsche ich die Dualität, die dynamische Wechselwirkung zwischen voneinander abhängigen Gegensätzen, und die Rätsel und Zweideutigkeiten, Konflikte und Harmonien, die sich aus der Beziehung der Gegensätze ergeben. Dualität wird oft durch das orientalische Symbol des Yin und Yang

( 78)

Judy SCHUSTER
U.S.A.

Assisted by DONNA HORST

Suspicious Fire at the Lost Dutchman Mine
Feux Suspects dans la Mine Perdue de l'Hollandais
Verdächtiges Feuer in der Mine des vermissten Holländers
78 x 63″ 198 x 160cm

KEVIN OLDS

Lilian TYRELL
U.S.A.

"Suspicious Fire at the Lost Dutchman Mine" is the first tapestry of a series called "Disaster Blankets". They depict storm damage, sabotaged airplanes, burning oil tankers, terrorist, Ku Klux Klan rallies, and scenes of war and destruction.

"Feu Suspect dans la Mine Perdue de l'Hollandais" est la première tapisserie d'une série qui s'appelle "Couvertures du Désastre". Toutes ces tapisseries dépeignent des dégâts provoqués par les orages, des sabotages d'avions, des pétroliers en feu, des terro-

"Suspicious Fire at the Lost Dutchman Mine" (verdächtiges Feuer in der Mine des vermissten Holländers) ist der erste Wandteppich in einer Serie, die sich "Disaster Blankets" (Katastrophendecken) nennt. Die Serie handelt von Sturmschäden, sabo-

(▶ 79)

Hall of the Lost Years
Le Salon des Annees Perdues
Die Halle der verlorenen Schritte
32 x 39″ 81 x 99cm

While opening a newspaper and seeing a photo of our Congress (Legislative Power Palace) I felt that many things converged inside myself. Mentally I was mixing remembrances, emotions, etc. with technical problems of weaving.

A moment arrived when the impression of joining the colour and the texture of wool with the idea, was growing to reality.

Lorsque j'ai vu dans un journal une photo de notre "Palacio Legislativo" (Palais Legislatif), j'ai été prise par une confusion de sentiments. Des souvenirs, des émotions, se sont mentalement mélangés à des problèmes techniques propres du tissage. A un moment donné l'assemblage de l'idée, du thème de l'ouvrage avec la couleur et la texture de la laine est devenu réalité.

Beim Aufschlagen einer Tageszeitung sah ich eine Bildaufnahme unseres Kongressgebäudes. Dabei empfand ich, dass Vieles auf mich zukam. Im Geist mischen sich Erinnerungen, Gefühle und so Manches mehr. In mir entstand der Drang, dieses in meiner Textilsprache zu gestalten.

Die Verbindung von Farbe und Wollstruktur mit dem Leitmotiv verwirklichte sich allmählich.

( 79)

Rosa ZIEGLER
Uruguay

EUROPEAN TAPESTRY TODAY

Now that we know the identity of the "Lady with the Unicorn" and may address her by her title, now that every antique tapestry has been recognized for its historical value, now that we see tapestry again in many modern buildings as the most beautiful, decorative contribution to architecture it is surprising that tapestry is generally still considered "merely" a craft and regarded as obsolete. In the last two decades there was a decline in European tapestry— it was not considered an autonomous artform anymore. Meanwhile there are increasing signs indicating a new rise ahead. Why was there a decline? And what is causing the revival?

The great innovator of tapestry art and its best advocate, Jean Lurçat, captured the interest in tapestry of the entire art world during the last 30 years of his life. After his death in 1966 the decline of the largest tapestry center (Aubusson in France) began due to a loss of clients and diminished interest in tapestry. Many of the most well known manufacturers had to close, among them the most famous "Tabard Soeurs et Freres", but also the "Munchenener Gobelin Manufaktur" (1985). The former clients were now looking for other artforms to embellish their architectural projects.

Time consuming work demands its price. Merely an offshoot of tapestry, handwoven textile products reached a larger buyer's market. Unfortunately tapestries soon ended up in the same category with the handwoven products and were dismissed as "crafts".

Surprisingly, the revival of tapestry began due to renewed interest and studies of ancient tapestry art. In earlier times tapestry had to fulfill societal needs. It made political statements and recounted mythological and religious stories with imagery in large formats. For instance, the most famous tapestry of the Renaissance is the "Lady with the Unicorn", whose puzzle was just recently solved by Andre Arnaud from Aubusson.[1] The myth of the unicorn, especially as portrayed on tapestry, is being revived. All over Europe we are witnessing the establishment of new but small tapestry workshops. Individual weavers, dyers and designers are exhibiting together and stimulating renewed interest in tapestry. The most famous museums are buying modern tapestries for their collections. Tapestry is also shown at numerous textile art exhibits (unfortunately not at the so-called "International Tapestry Biennal" of Lausanne). Tapestry is being considered an original art form once again.

LA TAPISSERIE EUROPÉENE D'AUJOURD'HUI

Maintenant que nous connaissons l'identité de la "Dame à la Licorne" et que nous pouvons lui faire référence par son titre, maintenant que chaque tapisserie antique a été reconnue pour sa valeur historique, maintenant que l'on reconsidère la tapisserie dans beaucoup de bâtiments modernes comme la contribution à l'architecture la plus belle et la plus décorative, il est surprenant que la tapisserie soit encore généralement simplement considerée comme une activité artisanale et plutot démodée. La tapisserie européenne est en déclin depuis les vingt dernières années. Elle n'est plus considérée comme un art autonome. Il y a de plus en plus de signes qui indiquent sa popularité croissante. Pourquoi y a-t-il eu un déclin et qu'est-ce qui explique cette résurrection?

Le grand innovateur de l'art de la tapisserie et son meilleur défenseur, Jean Lurçat a réussi à intéresser le monde entier à la tapisserie pendant les dernières trente années de sa vie. Après sa mort, en 1966, le déclin du plus grand centre de tapisserie, Aubusson en France, a commencé dû à un manque de clients et au peu d'intérêt pour la tapisserie. Beaucoup des ateliers les plus célèbres durent fermer, parmi eux le plus renommée "Tabard Soeurs et Frères", mais aussi le "Munchenener Goblein Manufaktur" (1985). Les anciens clients recherchaient maintenant d'autres formes d'art pour embellir leurs projets architecturaux.

Un travail long exige un prix élevé. A peine apparentés à la tapisserie, les produits textiles tissés à la main ont touché un marché plus large. La tapisserie a connu la malchance de se voir placée dans la même catégorie que les produits tissés à la main et de se voir ravaler au rang d'activité artisanale.

De façon surprenante, le renouveau de la tapisserie est dû à un regain d'intérêt pour l'art de la tapisserie ancienne. Dans le passé, la tapisserie devait remplir les besoins de la société. Elle représentait des prises de position politique et racontait des histoires mythologiques et religieuses avec des images à grands formats. Par exemple la plus célèbre tapisserie de la Renaissance est la "Dame à la Licorne" dont l'énigme vient seulement d'être résolue par André Arnaud d'Aubusson. (1) Le mythe de la licorne, en particulier comme il transparait en tapisserie, connait une seconde jeunesse. Dans toute l'Europe se créent de nouveaux petits ateliers de tapisserie. Des tisseurs individuels, des teinturiers, des compositeurs exposent ensemble et stimulent un regain d'intérêt pour la tapisserie. Les musées les plus célèbres achètent des tapisseries modernes pour leurs collections. Des tapisseries sont également montrées lors de nombreuses expositions d'art textile (malheureusement non à la soi-disant Réunion Internationale de Tapisserie biannuelle de Lausanne). La tapisserie une fois de plus se voit replacée parmi les arts.

EUROPÄISCHE TAPISSERIE HEUTE

Heute, da wir die Identität der "DAME mit EINHORN" kennen und sie mit ihrem Titel anreden können, heute, da jede antike Tapisserie in ihrem kunsthistorischen Wert anerkannt ist, heute da wir in vielen modernen Gebäuden wieder TAPISSERIE als den schönsten, dekorativen Beitrag zur Architektur sehen, wundert es, dass Tapisserie im allgemeinen immer noch als "nur" Kunsthandwerk abgetan und als obsolet angesehen wird. In den letzten beiden Jahrzehnten gab es einen Verfall der europäischen Tapisserie, man sah sie nicht mehr als eigenständige Kunstform an. Inzwischen mehren sich die Anzeichen, dass ein neuer Aufschwung kommt. Warum gab es den Verfall? Und was verursacht die Wiederbelebung?

Der grosse Erneuerer der Tapisseriekunst und ihr bester Fürsprecher, Jean LURÇAT, hielt während der letzten dreissig Jahre seines Lebens die gesamte Kunstwelt an der Tapisserie interessiert. Mit seinem Tod 1966 begann mit dem Verlust der Auftraggeber und des allgemeinen Interesses für die Tapisserie auch der Verfall des grössten Tapisserie-Zentrums, AUBUSSON in Frankreich. Viele der bekanntesten Manufakturen mussten schliessen, darunter die berühmteste "Tabard Soeurs et Freres", aber auch die "Münchener Gobelin Manufaktur" (1985). Die früheren Auftraggeber suchten sich andere Kunstformen für ihre Architektur-Bereicherungen.

Die zeitraubende Arbeit verlangt ihren Preis. Lediglich ein "Ableger" der Tapisserie, erreichten die handgesponnenen Textilerzeugnisse des Kunstgewerbes eine grössere Käuferschicht. Leider wurden Tapisserien bald in einen Topf mit den Handwebprodukten geworfen und auch als "Kunstgewerbe" abgetan.

Erstaunlicherweise begann die Wiederbelebung der Tapisserie dank des Interesses und der Studien an alter Tapisseriekunst. In früheren Zeiten hatte die Tapisserie gesellschaftliche Aufträge zu erfüllen. Sie machte politische Aussagen und erzählte bildhaft in Grossformaten Geschichten der Mythologie und der Religion. Die bekannteste Tapisserie der Renaissance z.B. ist die "DAME mit dem EINHORN", deren Geheimnis erst kürzlich enträtselt wurde durch Andre ARNAUD aus Aubusson[1]. Der Mythos vom Einhorn, vor allem in Tapisserie gewirkt, lebt wieder auf. Wir beobachten in ganz EUROPA die Gründung neuer, wenngleich kleiner Tapisserie-Werkstätten. Einzelne Wirker, Färber und Entwerfer stellen zusammen aus und beleben das Interesse an Tapisserie erneut. Die berühmtesten Museen erwerben moderne Tapisserie für ihre Sammlungen. In zahlreichen Textilkunst-Ausstellungen wird auch Tapisserie gezeigt (leider nicht in der sogenannten "Internationalen TAPISSERIE-Biennale" von Lausanne). Tapisserie wird wieder als eine originale Kunstform anerkannt. Man erkennt an, dass "Tapisserie"

One acknowledges that "tapisser" means to cover walls or to cover furniture with fabric—it is a functional term. Therefore the most important task is to preserve the ancient technique and to continue to teach its pecularities and rules in workshops and art schools. There cannot be a Renaissance of tapestry as it existed under Jean Lurçat whose 100th birthday will be celebrated in 1992. However, it is our duty as tapestry artists to open up new dimensions through innovation in the design of tapestry. With the resurrected UNICORN awakens the old and eternally young ART of TAPESTRY.

Dirk Holger

[1] They were woven in 1514, the Lady was "Mary of England"—"Duchess of Suffolk"—sister of Henry VIII and wife of Louis XII of France.

On s'accorde à reconnaître que "tapisser" signifie couvrir des murs ou des meubles avec du tissu—c'est un terme foncionnel. De ce fait la tâche la plus importante est de préserver la technique ancienne et de continuer à enseigner les règles et subtilités dans des ateliers et des écoles d'art. Il ne peut pas y avoir une renaissance de la tapisserie comme elle existait sous Jean Lurçat dont le centième anniversaire sera célébré en 1992. Néanmoins, c'est notre devoir d'artistes en tapisserie d'ouvrir de nouvelles dimensions pour l'innovation du dessin de la tapisserie. Avec la licorne ressuscitée s'éveille le viel art de la tapisserie, un art éternellement jeune.

Dirk Holger

(1) Elles ont été tissées en 1514. La Dame était "Marie d'Angleterre"—"Duchesse de Suffolk"—sœur d'Henry VIII et femme de Louis XII de France.

in erster Linie eine TECHNIK am Webstuhl ist. Das frz. "tapisser" bedeutet Wände bedecken oder Möbel bespannen, ist also ein funktionaler Begriff. Darum ist die wohl wichtigste Aufgabe, die uralte Technik zu bewahren und ihre Besonderheiten und Gesetze in Werkstätten und Kunstschulen weiter zu lehren. Eine Renaissance der Tapisseriekunst wie unter Jean LURÇAT, dessen hundertster Geburtstag 1992 gefeiert wird, kann es nicht geben. Aber unsere Aufgabe als Tapisseriekünstler ist es, durch Innovation der Gestaltung der Wandteppichkunst neue Dimensionen zu erobern. Mit dem wiederauferstandenen EINHORN erwacht auch wieder die alte und ewig junge KUNST der TAPISSERIE.

Dirk Holger

[1] Die "Dame" war Königin von Frankreich für nur drei Monate, ihr Titel ist in der Widmung "A mon seul Desir" enthalten.

Layering
Faire des couches
Schichtung
67 x 53″   170 x 135cm

Evelyn
GYRCIZKA
Austria

The freedom that defines itself makes us anticipate the future because structured thinking allows for an expanded visualisation of ideas. The abstract or non-objective world is a world of action and the preparation for artificiality which we always hope for.

Oswald Oberhuber

La liberté qui se définit nous laisse présager de l'avenir parce que la pensée structurée permet l'expansion visuelle des idées. Le monde abstrait ou non objectif est un monde d'action et la préparation à l'artificialité qu'on espère toujours.

Oswald Oberhuber

Die sich formulierende Freiheit versetzt uns in Erwartung der Zukunft, denn, strukturierendes Denken ermoglicht eine erweiterte Begriffsvorstellung. Das Abstrakte oder die ungegenstandliche Welt ist eine Welt des Handelns und die Vorbereitung auf die Kunstlichkeit, die wir doch immer erhoffen.

Oswald Oberhuber

Or Not
Ou pas
Oder Nicht
57 x 63″ 145 x 160cm

Words to my work:
The secrets of (individual?) myths and symbols
. . . of (the own?) life and death; to cultivate the (own?) mythology.
Fragile, ephemeral life . . .
Life *and* death
to be *and* not to be
illusion
Heart, fruit, tree, hand . . . as absolute beings;
. . . and the go between . . .
childhood?
The tissue speaks.

Quelques mots sur mon travail:
Les secrets des mythes et des symboles (individuels?)
. . . de la vie et de la mort (de chacun); afin de cultiver sa (propre?) mythologie.
Vie fragile et éphémère
Vie et mort
être et ne pas être
illusion

Coeur, fruit, arbre, main . . . comme des êtres absolus;
. . . et les intermédiaires . . .
l'enfance?
L'ouvrage tissé parle.

Die Geheimnisse (individueller?) Mythen und Symbole

. . . des (eigenen?) Lebens und Todes; die (eigene?) Mythologie kultivieren.

Zerbrechliches, vergängliches Leben . . .
Leben und Tod
Sein und Nicht-Sein
Schein

Herz, Frucht, Baum, Hand . . . als absolute Wesen;
. . . und die Beziehungen zueinander . . .
Kindheit?
Das Gewebe spricht.

Carmen
RAMIREZ
Austria

Sahara 2
71 x 49″ 180 x 125cm

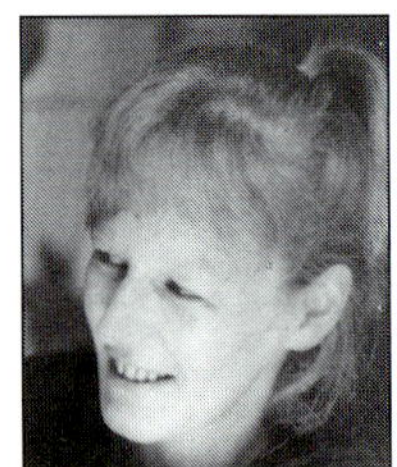

Christiana WUSTINGER
Austria

In the beginning there is the drawing, the design—why bother weaving? Weaving is important to me as a balance between mind and handwork; the urge for both is simultaneously satisfied. My works are "abstract"; the figurative simply emerges—it can be discovered in it. The painterly is dominated by the graphic, the symbol, the writing. The theme, unknown to me, is manifested, recognized, remembered in the work itself. I choose light foundations to

Au départ, il y a l'ébauche, le dessin—alors pourquoi y ajouter le tissage? A mon avis, il sert à rétablir un équilibre important entre le travail de l'esprit et le travail manuel; je satisfais en même temps ces deux besoins. Mes oeuvres sont "abstraites"; leur caractère métaphorique se révèle simplement—on peut le découvrir facilement. La partie peinte est dominée par la partie graphique, symbolique, écrite. Le thème, qui m'est inconnu, se manifeste, se recon-

Am Anfang ist die Zeichnung, der Entwurf—warum noch weben? Weben ist mir wichtig als Gleichgewicht zwischen Kopf-und Handwerk; das Bedürfnis nach beidem wird simultan befriedigt. Meine Arbeiten sind "abstrakte"; Figurales ergibt sich einfach, kann darin entdeckt werden. Malerisches wird vom Grafischen, dem Zeichen, der Schrift überwogen, das "Thema", mir unbewusst, in der Arbeit erst manifest, erkannt, wiedererkannt. Ich wähle helle

(▶ 79)

Lady on Red Chair
Femme sur chaise rouge
Dame auf rotem Stuhl
61 x 41"   155 x 105cm

Liev Beuten opts for an illustrative making up of figures, groups and situations from her own reality and interests on the understanding that the cartoon or design indicates to her the main lines and the planes, while she, by twisting together the kinds of wool, lets the picture organically grow without an

Liev Beuten-Schellekens choisit pour ses tapisseries une élaboration illustrée de figures, groupes et situations prises dans sa propre réalité et ses propres intérêts, sous cette réserve que le carton ou l'esquisse ne lui indique que les grandes lignes, alors qu'elle donne une vie organique à son tableau à

Liev Beuten-Schellekens optiert in ihren Wandeppichen für eine illustrative Verarbeitung von Figuren, Gruppen und Situationen aus ihrer eigenen Realität und ihrem eig'nem Interesse mit der Einschränkung dasz der karton oder Entwurf ihr die groszen Linien und Flächen heruberreicht, indem sie beim

(▶ 74)

Liev
BEUTEN
Belgium

The City
La ville
Die Stadt
79 x 55"   200 x 140cm

Marika SZARAZ
Belgium

I created a series of tapestries motivated by childhood memories and family influence. Remembering arm-chair covers, protective rugs over persian rugs, little flannel wraps around valuable items, I decided to create my own textile superimposition. I refer to feelings against lies, hypocrisy, pretense and outward appearance of family life. Words such as "hide" and "protect" overlap and merge becoming a symbol of a previous experience.

L'influence de souvenirs d'enfance, la mentalité familiale m'a poussée à créer une série de tapisseries qui évoquent pour moi les housses des fauteuils, la deuxième couche de tapis qui protégeaient les tapis persans, les petites pochettes de flanelle qui enveloppaient les objets de valeur, autant de types de superposition de tissus que je recrée à ma manière. Sont évoqués parallèlement une série de sentiments contre le mensonge, l'hypocrisie, le

Ich habe eine Tapisserieserie entworfen, die Kindheitserinnerungen und den Lebensstil meiner Familie ausdrückt. Die Erinnerung an Sesselschutzhauben, Schonteppiche über Persischen Teppichen, kleine Flanelletuis für Wertgegenstände hat mich dazu bewogen, meine eigene "Textilschichtung" zu entwerfen. Ich vermittle Gefühle gegenüber von Lügen, Heuchelei, Vortäuschung und dem äusserlichen Anschein des Familienlebens. Worte wie "vers-

(▶ 78)

Corps Celeste
67 x 75"   170 x 190cm

My main field of activity is tapestry weaving, where the characteristics and the surface structure of the technique create a basis for the concentration in black/white tapestries with strong graphic character in a constructive idiom.

Mon principal domaine d'activité est le tissage où les caracteristiques de la tapisserie et la structure superficielle de la technique créent une base pour la concentration de la tapisserie en noir et blanc avec un caractère graphique très fort d'un idiome constructif.

Meine Hauptbeschäftigung ist Tapisserieweben. Beim Weben wird durch die Struktur der Oberfläche und die Webmethode eine Basis geschaffen für schwarzweisse Tapisserien mit starkem graphischen Charakter und tiefer Ausdruckskraft.

Anet
BRUSGAARD
Denmark

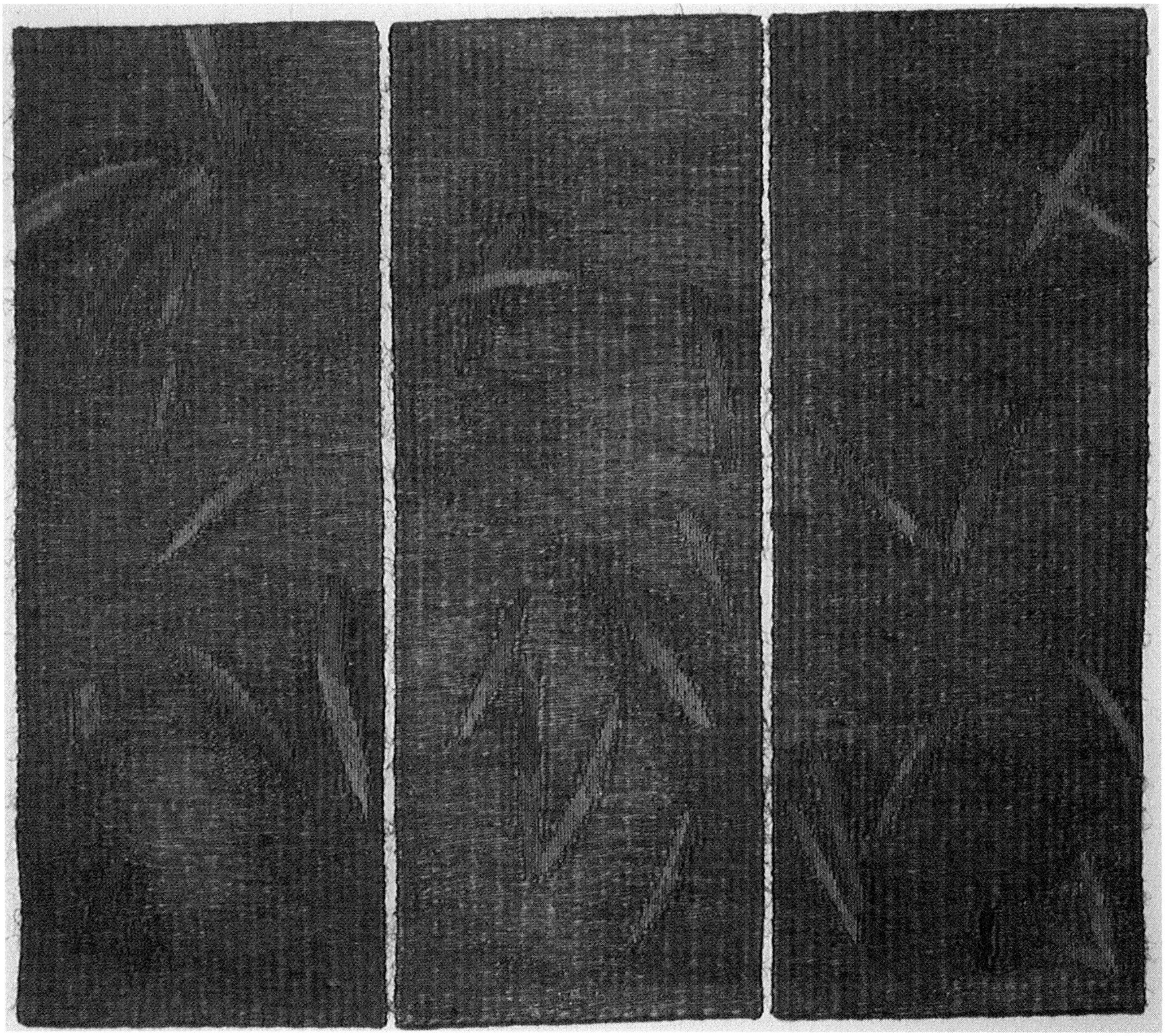

Untitled
Sans Nom
Ohne Titel
38 x 47" 97 x 120cm

Lisbeth GRAEM
Denmark

The tapestry is a preliminary work in a competition towards the commission for a decoration of the Danish Hall of Parliament.

As the hall is large and architecturally incoherent it was essential for me through colours and lines to create harmony with my tapestry. The full scale tapestry was never executed. The materials used are: sisal and linen.

Cette tapisserie représente l'étape préliminaire d'un projet présenté à la commission chargée de la décoration du Hall du Parlement Dancis.

Comme le Hall est vaste et d'architecture incohérente, il était essentiel pour moi d'utiliser les couleurs et les lignes au service de l'harmonie de ma tapisserie. Cette tapisserie n'a jamais été exécutée à son echelle réelle. Les matériaux utilisés ici sont les fibres de sisal et le lin.

Diese Tapisserie ist ein Entwurf für einen Wettbewerb um den Auftrag zur Dekoration der dänischen Parlamentshalle.

Da die Halle sehr gross ist und keinerlei architektonische Harmonie aufweist, stellte sich mir das Problem, durch Farben und Linien in meiner Tapisserie Harmonie zu erzeugen. Die Tapisserie wurde nicht in vollem Maβstab angefertigt. Die verwendeten Materialien sind Sisal und Leinen.

Credit
Kredit
24 x 39" 61 x 99cm

My work is concerned with technology and the man made environment. I am interested in images which illustrate man's use and misuse of technology; images which reflect something of life in this century.

I feel that tapestry is an appropriate medium through which to explore these images. As an ancient craft and something which is completely hand made, it contrasts vividly with the images of 20th century

Mes travaux sont orientés vers la technologie et l'environnement créé par l'homme. Je m'intéresse aux images qui montrent que l'homme use et abuse de la technologie: images qui projettent quelque chose de la vie à notre époque.

Je crois que la tapisserie est un moyen d'expression approprié à l'exploration de ces images. L'ancienneté de cet artisanat où tout est fait à la main s'oppose d'une manière frappante aux images de

Meine Arbeit befasst sich mit der Technologie und mit der vom Menschen manipulierten Umwelt. Mich interessieren Motive, die den Gebrauch und Missbrauch der Umwelt durch den Menschen illustrieren; Motive, die etwas über das Leben in diesem Jahrhundert aussagen.

Für mich ist Tapisserie ein geeignetes Medium zur Erforschung dieser Motive. Als ein uraltes Gewerbe und als etwas völlig Handgearbeitetes, bietet es

(▶ 74)

Sue BECKETT
England

Princess Di meets a Medieval Maiden
Rencontre de Princesse Di et de la Jeune Fille Medievale
Prinzessin Di begegnet einer Jungfrau aus dem Mittelalter
38 x 42″   97 x 107cm

Invited Artist
Archie BRENNAN
England

Some years ago, I was weaving a quite large area of plain black when some men set off for the moon. They got there before I was finished.

I work in a minor art form. Tapestry is an indulgent, elitist, economically farcical, and frequently boring 20th century activity.

Il y a quelques années, alors que j'étais en train de tisser une pièce de bonne taille de couleur noire, quelques hommes entreprenaient un voyage vers la lune. Ils y arrivèrent avant que je ne finisse.

Mon travail fait partie des arts mineurs. Au vingtième siècle, la tapisserie est une activité indulgente, élitiste, souvent ennuyeuse et comique d'un point de vue économique.

Vor einigen Jahren, als ein paar Männer zum Mond geflogen sind, webte ich eine ziemlich grosse Fläche in einfachem schwarz. Sie erreichten ihr Ziel, bevor ich meine Arbeit beendet hatte.

Ich arbeite in einer minderen Kunstform. Tapisserie ist eine befriedigende, elitäre, ökonomisch lachhafte und oftmals langweilige Beschäftigung des 20. Jahrhunderts.

(▶ 74)

Untitled
Sans Nom
Ohne Titel
72 x 62"   182 x 157cm

My work is almost autobiographical, derived from events and objects taken from my daily life, things that make an impression on me and stir me up in some way.

The work is a celebration of fertility and womanhood encompassing many ideas, natural rhythms, my travels to other countries and a liking for collected objects.

Mon travail est presque autobiographique. Il découle des événements, des objets pris dans ma vie de tous les jours et des choses qui me laissent une impression ou qui m'émeuvent d'une certaine manière.

Mon travail célèbre la fertilité et la féminité et embrasse de nombreuses idées, des rythmes naturels, mes voyages à l'étranger et l'amour que j'ai à collectionner des objets.

Meine Werke sind biographisch, indem sie Objekte und Ereignisse meines täglichen Lebens wiederspiegeln. Meine Arbeit befasst sich mit Dingen, die mich beeindrucken und auf irgendeine Weise berühren.

Mein Werk ist ein Triumph der Fruchtbarkeit und Weiblichkeit. Es umfasst viele verschiedene Konzepte, natürliche Rhythmen, meine Reisen in andere Länder und meine Vorliebe für gesammelte Objekte.

(▶ 75)

Shelly
GOLDSMITH
England

He who loves writes on walls
Celui qui aime ecrit sur les murs
Wer liebt, der schreibt auf Mauern
78 x 54″ 198 x 137cm

Tass
MAVROGORDATO
England

My work uses traditional methods of tapestry weaving and figurative subject matter. The juxtapositioning of images as well as selective use of colour go to create symbolic and representational compositions. Inspiration is drawn from the human figure, urban environments and literature.

Dans mon travail je me sers des méthodes traditionnelles de tapisserie tissée et de sujets figuratifs. La juxtaposition des images aussi bien que le choix des couleurs concourent à créer des compositions symboliques et représentatives. Je m'inspire de la figure humaine, de l'environnement urbain et de la littérature.

In meiner Arbeit verwende ich traditionelle Methoden des Tapisseriewebens und bildliche Motive. Durch gezielte Farbwahl und das Nebeneinanderstellen von Motiven entstehen symbolische sowie auch gegenständliche Kompositionen. Für Inspiration sorgen der menschliche Körper, das Stadtleben und die Literatur.

From the Indian Empire
En provenance de l'Empire Indien
Aus dem Reich der Inder
26 x 26" 66 x 66cm

I want people to look at my work and know what to *feel* and not what to *think*. Tapestry is my medium because it can incorporate movement, colour gesture and a particular resonance that is quite unique. And, of course, I do have enormous relish for the strength and beauty of the finished product.

Je veux que les gens regardent mon travail en sachant que *sentir* et non que *penser*. La tapisserie est ma méthode d'expression parce qu'elle offre la possibilité d'incorporer mouvement, couleur, geste et une résonance particulière qui est assez unique. Et bien entendu, j'éprouve un enorme plaisir devant la force et la beauté du produit fini.

Ich möchte, dass man mein Werk betrachtet und erkennt, was man *fühlen* soll und nicht, was man *denken* soll. Tapisserie ist mein Medium, weil es auf einzigartige Weise Bewegung, Farbe, Geste und gewisse Resonanz vereinigt. Und natürlich freue ich mich über die Stärke und Schönheit des fertigen Produktes.

Invited Artist
Marta ROGOYSKA
England

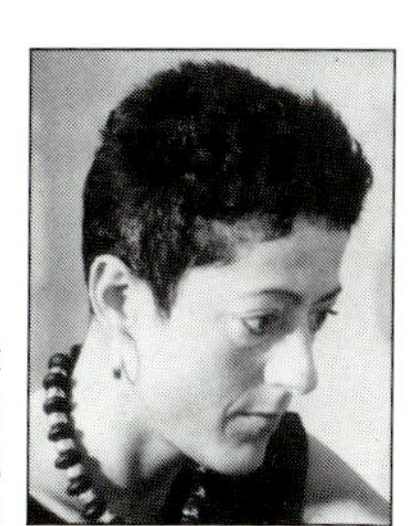

PETER COOPER

The Architecture Shop
L'Atelier d'Architecture
Das Architekturgeschäft
51 x 47″ 130 x 119cm

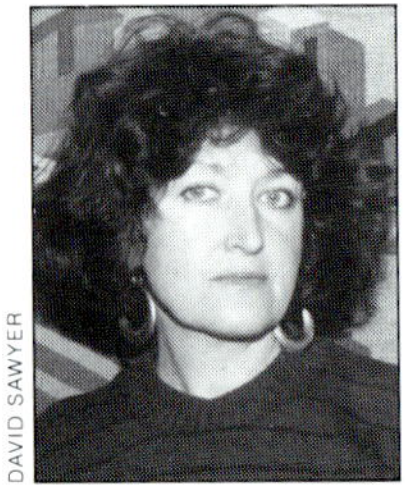

DAVID SAWYER

Christine SAWYER
England

I am fascinated by the relationship between freedom and restriction in tapestry—the challenge being to make fresh vital images in this rather rigid process—working from the bottom up, back to front, thinking so far ahead.

Je suis fascinée par la relation entre la liberté et la restriction de la tapisserie—la gageure étant de fabriquer des images fraiches et vivantes à l'aide d' un procédé plutot rigide—en travaillant du bas vers le haut, de l'arrière vers l' avant, en prévoyant longtemps à l'avance.

Mich fasziniert das Verhältnis zwischen Freiheit und Einschränkung in der Tapisserie—es fordert mich dazu heraus, innerhalb dieses starren Rahmens frische vitale Motive zu entwerfen und von unten nach oben, von hinten nach vorne zu arbeiten und vorauszuplanen.

(▶ 78)

Yellow Wall Piece
Pan de Mur Jaune
Gelber Wandbehang
71 x 78″   180 x 198cm

Dilys
STINSON
England

It is only in the last year that I have been able to work on larger pieces, and I love it. For me the tapestries work best on a large scale.

The designs are first worked out in collages of handmade and commerically-produced paper, some painted or dyed, cut and torn. These are translated into weaving. I like to use different fibres to interpret the different surfaces of the paper, using silk, cotton,

Je ne suis capable de travailler sur de plus grandes pièces que depuis l'anñee dernière et j'aime ça. A mon avis, il vaut mieux faire des tapisseries sur une grande échelle.

On développe d'abord les ébauches avec des collages de papier fait-main ou commercial qui peut être peint ou teint, coupé ou déchiré. Celles-ci sont transposées au tissage. J'aime utiliser des fibres

Erst seit dem letzten Jahr habe ich die Gelegenheit, an grösseren Werken zu arbeiten und ich tue es mit Begeisterung. Mir gelingen Tapisserien am besten in Grossformat.

Die Entwürfe werden zunächst in Collagen mit kommerziellem und selbsthergestelltem Papier ausgearbeitet. Das selbstgemachte Papier wird gefärbt oder bemalt, zerschnitten und zerrissen. Ich benutze

(▶ 78)

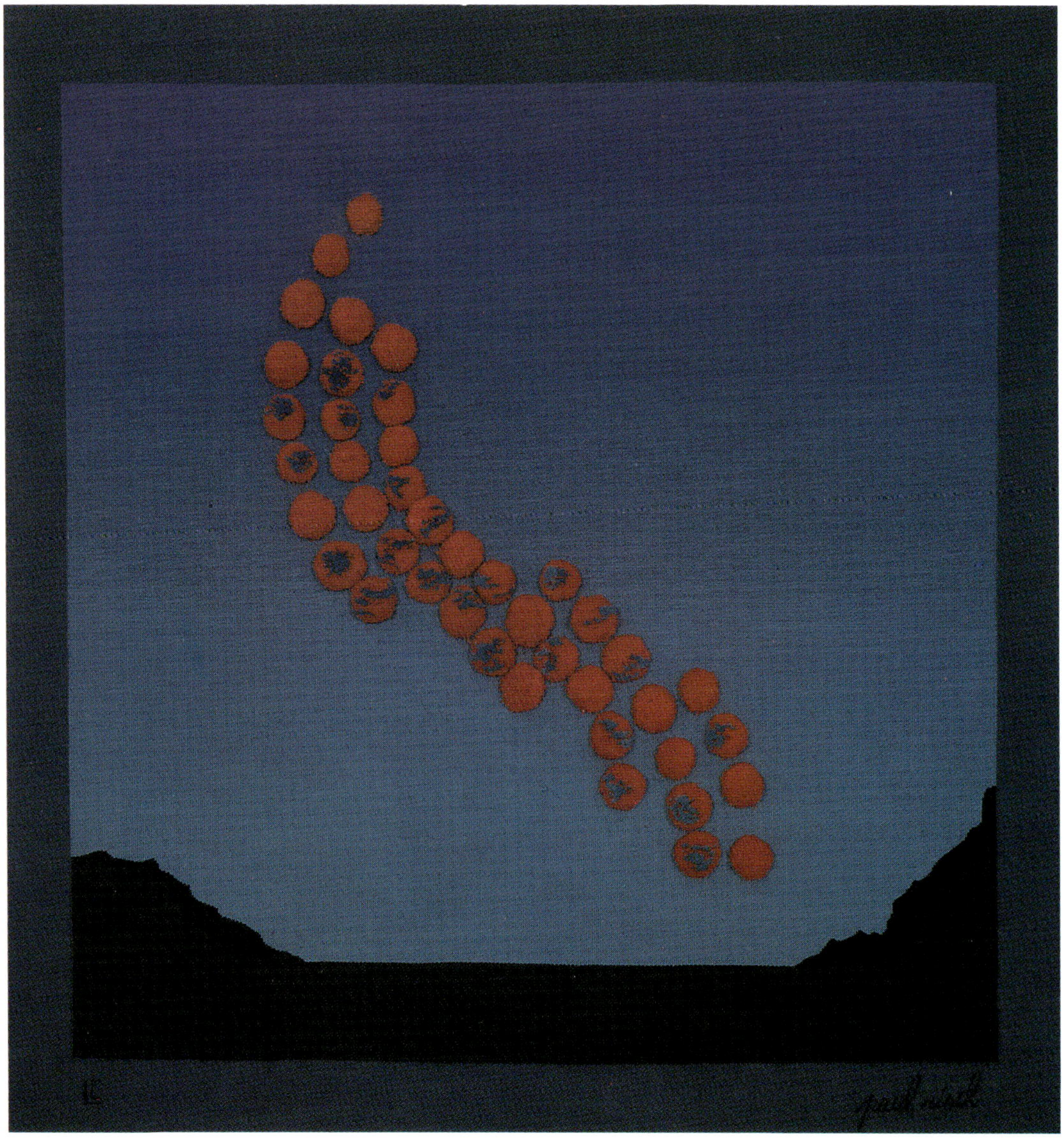

Flying cakes in the morning
Gateaux volants au petit matin
Fliegender Kuchen am Morgen
63 x 63″ 160 x 160cm

Invited Artist
Paul
RISCH
France

Tapestry is a way to weave clothes for my dreams.

La tapisserie est un moyen de tisser l'habit de mes rêves.

Durch Tapisserie webe ich Kleidung für meine Träume.

Stag-Beetle
Cerf-volant
Hirschkafer
46 x 35″ 117 x 89cm

Once a butterfly flew into my room—when it perished, I mounted it on a pin. I stared at it for a long time—as I already admired other bugs as well. When I make a picture, I do not transform and stylize them—they are such perfect creatures that I have no right to falsify them.

Un papillon est entré dans ma chambre un jour—et je l'ai épinglé quand il est mort. Comme je m'intéressais déjà aux insectes, je l'ai admiré pendant longtemps.

Quand je reproduis des insectes, je refuse de les tranformer ou de les styliser—ces créatures sont si parfaites que je n'ai pas le droit de les dénaturer.

Es flatterte einmal ein Schmetterling in mein Zimmer—als er starb, habe ich ihn auf eine Nadel geheftet. Ich habe ihn mir lange angeschauht—schon damals habe ich Insekten bewundert.

Wenn ich Bilder entwerfe, verändere oder vereinfache ich die Form der Insekten nicht—sie sind solche perfekten Kreaturen, dass ich kein Recht darauf habe, sie zu verfälschen.

(▶ 77)

Judit NAGY
Hungary

Cabbages
Choux
Kohlkopfe
78 x 52" 198 x 132cm

M. MUSIAL

Barbara
FALKOWSKA
Poland

It is a consuming adventure: to make material the non-material. I translate into concrete substance that which is in me, in a non-material state. All that has been collected over a lifetime now acquires a material form.

Anthing can provide a subject because anything can be woven. Everything can be expressed with thread on a loom.

C'est une aventure de longue haleine de matérialiser ce qui est immatériel. Je transpose ce qui se trouve en moi dans un état immatériel en quelque chose de concret. Tout ce que j'ai acquis pendant ma vie prend alors une forme tangible.

Tous les sujets sont bons car tout peut être tissé. On peut tout exprimer sur un métier à tisser.

Es ist ein verzehrendes Abenteuer — dem Nicht-Materiellen eine Gestalt zu geben. Das, was in mir in nicht-materieller Form existiert, übertrage ich in eine konkrete Substanz. All das, was sich während meiner Lebenszeit angesammelt hat, wird nun in materieller Form ausgedrückt.

Alle möglichen Dinge verschaffen mir Inspiration, denn alles kann gewebt werden, alles kann mit der Faser am Webstuhl ausgedrückt werden.

(▶ 75)

Tapestry in Memory of my Mother
Tapisserie a la Memoire de ma Mere
Tapisserie in Erinnerung an meine Mutter
59 x 59"   150 x 150cm

Since the complicated process of weaving is made up of a number of fibre movements we cannot give any reason why should a tapestry have a flat printed-like surface. On the contrary, there is place for a melange of subtones and a mixture of fibres of different texturing; here I mean those of valours or painterly with the application of wool, cotton, silk, etc. I define it as "soft weaving". Such surface of the tapestry seems to be more interesting, richer, vivid and it does not mean that form has taken advantage over its content.

Les ouvrages de tapisserie ne se présentent pas comme des surfaces planes imprimees puisque le processus compliqué du tissage se fait à partir de l'agencement d'un certain nombre de fibres. Cela permet, bien au contraire, des mélanges de teintes et de fibres de textures différentes; je parle là des ouvrages de valeur et pleins de couleur qui se servent de laine, coton, soie, etc. Je lui donne le nom de "tissage en douceur". La surface de ce genre de tapisserie me parait plus intéressante, plus riche, plus éclatante sans que la forme prenne le pas sur le contenu.

Da das komplizierte Webverfahren aus etlichen Faserbewegungen besteht, gibt es keinen Grund, warum die Tapissereie eine flache "gedruckte" Oberfläche haben sollte. Im Gegenteil, es gibt viel Spielraum für eine Reihe von Farbnuancen und Fasermischungen mit verschiedenen Mustern. Ich spreche von einer malartigen Anwendung von Wolle, Baumwolle, Seide etc. Ich nenne es "sanftes Weben". Diese Art der Flächengestaltung ist interessanter, vielseitiger und lebendiger, aber das bedeutet nicht, dass die Form den Inhalt überschattet.

(▶ 76)

Invited Artist
Aleksandra
MAŃCZAK
Poland

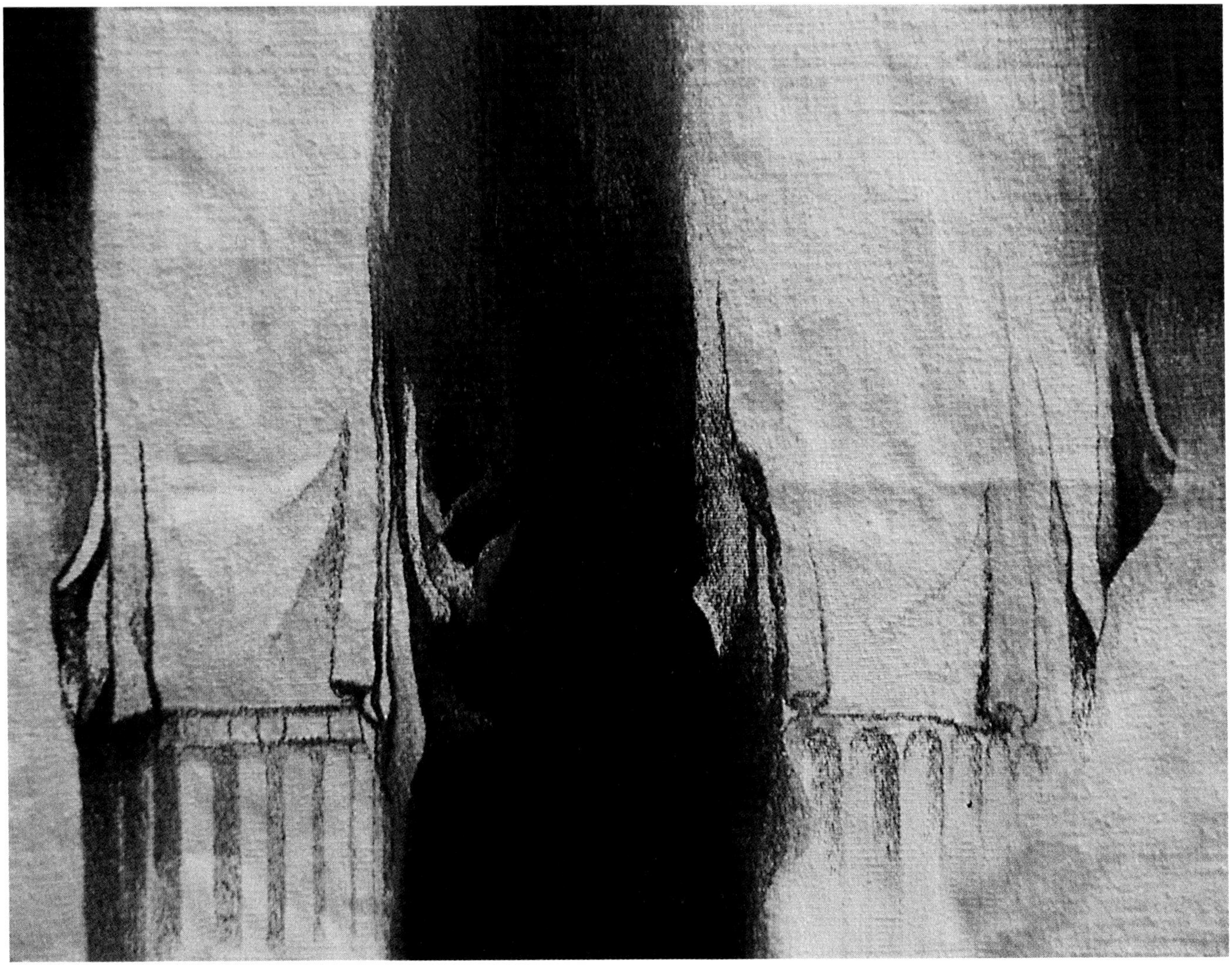

Demost
53 x 71"   135 x 180cm

Anna MICHNIEWICZ-SZERSZEŃ
Poland

In the last five to six years antiquity (especially Greek sculpture and architectural forms and mythological subjects) has been the general inspiration of my creative activity. I make use of it in gobelins and three-dimensional woven compositions. The main principle is the simplicity of the shape and the colour, that's why my works are generally achromatic. Besides that, my favorite colours are black and white.

Pendent les cinq ou six dernières années, l'antiquité (particulièrement le sculpture grecque, les formes architecturales et les sujets mythologiques) ont constitué la principale source d'inspiration de mon activité créatrice. Je l'utilise en gobelins et en compositions tissées en trois dimensions. Le principe général est la simplicité de la forme et de la couleur; c'est pourquoi mes œuvres sont généralement de deux couleurs. Je travaille le plus volontiers le noir et blanc.

In den letzten fünf bis sechs Jahren fand ich für meine kreative Tätigkeit Inspiration in der Antike (besonders griechische Skulptur, architektonische Formen und mythologische Themen). Ich verwende antike Motive in Gobelins und dreidimensionalen Kompositionen. Meine Werke sind zum grössten Teil achromatisch—ich betone Einfachheit in der Form und in der Farbe. Meine Lieblingsfarben sind schwarz und weiβ.

Untitled
Sans Nom
Ohne Titel
71 x 51″ 180 x 130cm

As a tapestry weaver I feel that "tapestry" is a collaboration of four units, each as exciting and important as the other. These units are: the idea, the drawing, the final design and the weaving. I could not give up my drawing for the weaving, nor my weaving for the drawing. Without each aspect there could be no finished work, the subject matter is as important as the finished work. Its statement is symbolic imagery which is all part of what gives tapestry and drawing its importance and life.

En tant que tisseuse, je pense que la "tapisserie" est la collaboration de quatre unités qui sont aussi importantes et passionnantes les unes que les autres. Ce sont l'idée, le dessin, le projet final et le tissage. Je ne voudrais pas laisser le dessin de côté pour le tissage ou vice versa. Le travail fini requiert chacun de ces aspects et le sujet traité est aussi important que le travail fini. Ce témoignage est rempli du symbolisme qui fait partie de chaque aspect de la tapisserie et du dessin et qui leur donne leur importance et leur vie.

Als Tapisseriweberin sehe ich "Tapisserie" als ein Zusammenwirken von vier Elementen. Jedes Element ist so aufregend und wichtig wie das Andere: die Idee, die Zichnung, der letzte Entwurf und das Weben. Ich könnte mein Zeichnen nicht für das Weben aufgeben und das Weben nicht für das Zeichnen. Ohne beide Aspekte gäbe es kein vollendetes Werk. Der Inhalt ist ebenso wichtig wie das vollendete Werk. Das symbolische Motiv spiegelt die Aussage wieder und das verleigt dem Weben Gewicht und Leben.

Sara BRENNAN
Scotland

The Seed and the Land
La Semence et la Terre
Die Saat und das Land
53 x 67″ 135 x 170cm

Lucy
TAYLOR
Scotland

"The ripe fruit rests here,
on the chill ground,
in the sterile air,
all meanings have fallen into your lap,
uncomprehending earth."

Edwin Muir 1887-1959

Tapestry has its own specific features and for me, it is the gradual emergence of a tactile image which holds the excitement. I have been interested in expressing visually the feelings which are sparked off through literature as well as the more accessible images of the land with the people and things which move in relation to it. I hope that the woven image will be at once recognisable and ambiguous.

"Le fruit mûr reste là, Sur le sol gelé, Dans l'air stérile, Le sens de toutes choses est tombé sur vos genoux, Terre qui ne comprend pas."

Edwin Muir 1887-1959

La tapisserie a ses propres caractéristiques: ce qui me passionne le plus c'est la formation progressive d'une image faite à la main. J'aime exprimer visuellement les sensations que la littérature éveille en moi ainsi que les images plus simples de la terre avec les gens et les choses qui lui sont étroitement liés. Je souhaite que l'image tissée soit identifiable à première vue tout en restant ambigüe.

"Die reife Frucht ruhet hier,
auf der kühlen Erde,
in der sterilen Luft.
Alle Bedeutungen sind in Deinen Schoss gefallen,
nicht verstehende Erde."

Edwin Muir 1887-1959

Die Tapisserie hat ihre besonderen Eigenheiten. Fur mich ist es das allmähliche Hervortreten eines fühlbaren Motivs, das mich reizt. Ich bin immer daran interessiert, visuell die Gefühle auszudrucken, die durch die Literatur inspiriert sind. Auch die alltäglichen Motive des Landes mit den Menschen und Dingen, die sich darin bewegen, sorgen für Inspiration. Ich hoffe, dass das gewebte Motiv gleichzeitig erkennbar und zweideutig ist.

Mid-winter Rite
Sacrifice du Solstice d'Hiver
Mittsommerzeremonie
63 x 75"   160 x 190cm

When weaving my tapestries my thoughts circulate round fundamental questions like life and death, birth and mortality, light and darkness. I pay homage to nature in its struggle against human technology, that threatens to make all life on our planet extinct. My questions are difficult questions, to which there are no definite answers. Consequently my tapestries can't give any definite answers either.

I leave it to the observer to make his own associations.

Lorsque je tisse mes images, mes pensées s'assemblent autour des questions fondamentales de la vie et de la mort, de la naissance et du dépérissement, de la lumière et de l'obscurité. Je rends une ovation à la Nature dans son combat contre la technologie humaine qui menace de destruction chaque vie sur notre planète. Mes questions sont des questions difficiles, auxquelles aucunes réponses simples et sans équivoque n'existent. C'est pourquoi mes images ne sont pas sans équivoques elles-mêmes. Je laisse à l'observateur de mes oeuvres la liberte dé faire ses propres associations.

Beim Weben meiner Bilder kreisen meine Gedanken über fundamentale Fragen wie Leben und Tod, Geburt und Vergänglichkeit, Licht und Dunkelheit. Ich fühle eine starke Verbindung zur Natur in ihrem Kampf gegen die menschliche Technologie, die jedes Leben auf unserem Planeten zu vernichten droht. Meine Fragen sind komplizierte Fragen, worauf es keine eindeutigen Antworten gibt. Folgenderweise sind meine Bilder nicht eindeutig. Ich überlasse es dem Betrachter seine eigenen Assoziationen zu machen.

Ulla
WERIN
Sweden

Fibersuns
Filaments de soleil
Fadensonnen
31 x 55″ 79 x 140cm

Margrit SUTTER-FURRER
Switzerland

My creations on the loom grow spontaneously. Only rarely do I use sketches or cartoons. I create sensed existence—I weave my thoughts and dreams into the form and emphasize my narration with color. I lose myself meditatively in my work.

I do not want to say anything about my work "Sonnendaden" (threads of sun). My wish is to let the work itself speak to the viewer.

Mes créations naissent spontanément sur le métier à tisser. Je me sers rarement d'esquisses ou de cartons. Je crée une existence sensible—Je donne une forme tissée à mes pensées et à mes rêves et je souligne mon récit avec des couleurs. Je me perds en méditation dans mon travail.

Je ne veux rien dire de mon travail "Sonnenfaden" (filaments de soleil). Je préfère que l'oeuvre parle d'elle-même à celui qui la regarde.

Meine Arbeiten am Webstuhl wachsen spontan. Nur selten verwende ich Skizze oder Karton.

Ich gestalte erfühltes Dasein—webe meine Gedanken und Träume in die Form und unterstreiche mein Erzählen mit Farbe. Meditativ verliere ich mich an mein Tun.

Über mein Werk "Sonnenfäden" möchte ich nichts berichten. Ich wünsche, dass sich der Besucher vom Werk selber ansprechen lasst.

FOTOSTUDIO SCHMIDT

Transmissions
Transmissionen
78 x 78″ 198 x 198cm

My tapestry "Transmission" represents the concept of electricity in our technological age. By using structural components as elements of its design I intended to record the time in which we live and to visualize its genius.

It has been a fascinating task for me to translate something technical into a totally different medium, textile.

Ma tapisserie "Transmission" représente la conception de l'électricite dans notre temps technique. En utilisant des pieces de construction comme élements de réalisation artistique, j'ai envisagé de tenir le temps dans lequel nous vivons et son esprit.

Convertir quelque chose de technique en un moyen entiérement différent, cela a été pour moi une expérience fascinante.

Tapisserie "Transmission—Elektrizität" In der Tapisserie "Transmission" versuche ich die Faszination moderner technischer Konstruktion als Ausdruck der Statik mit der Dynamik der Hochspannungselektrizitat zu einer Synthese zu vereinen. Kalte Metallteile mit scharfen Kanten überschneiden sich in spitzen Winkeln und verlieren sich in perspektivischen und farblichen Abstufungen, um damit das Spannungsverhältnis zwischen Materie und Energie auszudrücken.

( 74)

Ursula
BENKER-SCHIRMER
West Germany

Border
Bordure
Bordure
61 x 43"   156 x 110cm

Woven in Aubusson

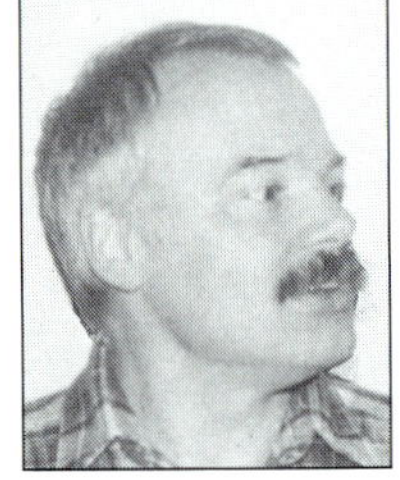

Invited Artist
Dirk HOLGER
West Germany

In 1959 I saw the very first tapestry in my life. It happened to be the largest single work by Jean Lurçat: "Wine, Musique and Poetry" (almost 100 sq. yds. on a black, cosmic background—in the Festival Hall of Cologne). Then and there I decided to become a tapestry artist. When in 1964 and 65 Jean Lurçat taught me the secrets of the spirit of tapestry designing I know that I made the right choice. Here is a statement of my former Latin teacher (Dr. Heinrich Hahne): "Anyone who is not thinking of tapestry by night and day does not exist for Holger." He is right.

En 1959 je vis une tapisserie pour la première fois de ma vie. L'œuvre se trouvait être la plus grande jamais exécutée par Jean Lurçat "Vin, Musique et Poesie," (de presque 100 mètres carré sur un fond cosmique dans le Palais des Festivals de Cologne). Sur le champ, je décidai de devenir un artiste en tapisserie. Quand en 1964 et 65 Jean Lurçat m'a enseigné les secrets de l'esprit du travail de la tapisserie, je sus que j'avais fait le bon choix. La déclaration suivante est de mon ancient professeur de Latin (Docteur Heinrich Hahne): "Quiconque ne pense pas à la tapisserie jour et nuit n'existe pas pour Holger." Il a raison.

1959 sah ich zum ersten Mal in meinem Leben eine Tapisserie. Es war Jean Lurçats gröβtes Werk "Wein, Musik und Gedichte", (fast 100 Quadratmeter auf schwarzem, kosmischen Untergrund—in der Kölner Festhalle). Genau zu dem Zeitpunkt entschied ich mich, Tapisseriekünstler zu werden. Als mich Jean Lurçat 1964 und 1965 über das Geheimnis des Tapisserieentwurfs aufklärte, wuβte ich, daβ ich mich richtig entschieden hatte. Es folgt eine Aussage meines ehemaligen Lateinlehrers (Dr. Heinrich Hahne): "Jemand, der nicht Tag und Nacht an Tapisserie denkt, existiert für Holger nicht". Er hat recht.

Tone
Son
Klang
75 x 55″   190 x 140cm

My work can be divided into two main themes. One is the presentation of correlations, of movements, of symbolized signs and relationships between powers. The other is the analogue configuration of musical themes.

Deux orientations dominent dans mes travaux. L'une se consacre au rationnel, aux rapports de force, aux mouvements et aux signes symboliques, l'autre, à la transposition morphologique de thèmes musicaux.

Zwei grosse Themenkreise bestimmen meine Arbeiten: zum einen die Darstellung von Beziehungen, Kräfteverhältnissen, Bewegungen und symbolhaften Zeichen, zum anderen die analoge Gestaltung musikalischer Themen.

(▶ 76)

Brigitte KRAMER-PETERS
West Germany

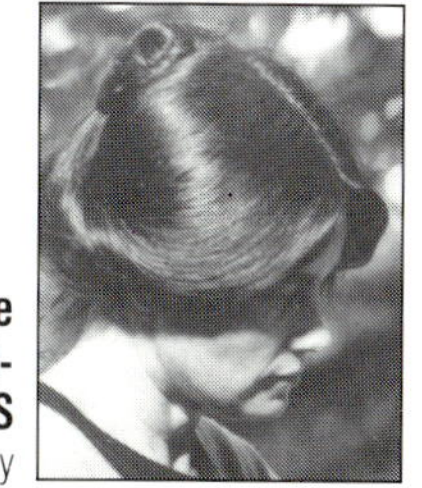

SUMMARY BY COUNTRY

	Registrations	Entrants	Entries	Accepted
Australia	36	13	18	4 (2*)
Austria	12	11	18	3
Belgium	6	3	6	2
Brazil	1	0	0	0
Canada	18	13	21	3 (2*)
Czechoslovakia	1	1	2	0
Denmark	24	12	18	2
Finland	3	1	2	0
France	18	13	24	0 (1*)
Germany, East	5	3	6	0
Germany, West	25	23	40	2 (1*)
Greece	1	0	0	0
Hungary	1	1	2	1
Iceland	2	1	2	0
Ireland	5	1	2	0
Japan	1	1	2	0
Korea	1	1	2	0
Netherlands	6	2	4	0
New Zealand	4	0	0	0 (1*)
Norway	4	2	3	0
Poland	5	5	8	2 (1*)
Portugal	2	1	1	0
Spain	2	0	0	0
Sweden	13	9	15	1
Switzerland	4	4	8	1
U.S.S.R				
Latvia	1	0	0	0
United Kingdom	45	20	34	5 (2*)
Scotland	4	2	4	2
United States	241	102	164	8 (3*)
Uruguay	4	4	6	1
	495	249	412	37+13=50

*Invited artists

Jurors:
Jenny Zimmer: Dean, School of Art & Design, Chisholm Institute of Technology, Victoria, Australia.
Marcel Marois: Professor of Tapestry, Painting and Drawing, University of Quebec, and University Laval, Quebec City, Canada.
Mary Farmer: Head of Tapestry Studio, Royal College of Art, London, England.
Paul Risch: Director, Ecole Nationale d'Art Décoratif d'Aubusson, Aubusson, France.

BECKETT

mass production. There is an irony in representing today's fast changing world of technology and consumerism, in this very permanent medium, with all its dignified traditions. By juxtaposing these ideas I hope to make people take a second look at these commonplace images and view them with fresh insight.

production en masse du vingtième siècle. Il y a une certaine ironie à représenter notre monde changeant et régi par la technologie et la consommation à travers une forme d'expression si permanente et pleine de traditions dignes.

Je juxtapose ces idées dans l'espoir que les gens regarderont de plus prés ces images de la vie de tous les jours et y découvriront quelque chose de nouveau.

einen lebendigen Kontrast zu den Motiven der Massenproduktion des 20. Jahrhunderts. Es ist etwas Ironisches dabei, wenn man die heutige, veränderliche Welt der Technologie und des Konsums in diesem permanenten Medium mit all seiner würdevollen Tradition festhält.

Durch die Juxtaposition dieser Motive hoffe ich, die Leute dazu anzuregen, einen weiteren Blick auf diese alltäglichen Objekte zu werfen und bei der Betrachtung einen neuen Eindruck zu gewinnen.

BENKER-SHIRMER

I playfully composed given structural rhythms and structures, which by their contrasting qualities and various nuances form an electric field, and which are to represent vibrating high tension.

The idea and the design of a tapestry require not only artistic intuition but also the technical skills of a devoted weaver to translate the artist's creative imagination and aesthetic ideas and intentions into its textile medium.

J'ai composé, à la legere, des rythmes de construction et des structures données, qui, par leurs qualités contraires et par des nuances variées, forment un champ électrique et doivent représenter une haute tension vibrante.

L'idée et le canevas d'un gobelin exigent non seulement de l'intuitiuon artistique mais aussi la compétence technique d'un tapissier plein de dévouement pour transposer l'imagination créatrice de l'artiste et ses idées et intentions esthétiques en son moyen textile.

Jahrzehntelang beschäftige ich mich mit dem Entwerfen und Weben von Tapisserien. Die Gestaltungselemente und Themen entstammen vorwiegend der Natur, z.B. Pflanzenformen oder Kristalle. Ich bevorzuge dabei gerne kräftige Farben.

Meine Auftraggeber sind vor allem Firmen, Banken und staatliche Institutionen, aber auch Privatpersonen. Neben meiner Entwurfstätigkeit betreibe ich eine kleine Gobelinmanufaktur mit sieben grossen und fünf kleinen Webstühlen, in der neben eigenen Entwürfen Gobelins für international bekannte Künstler gewebt werden.

BEUTEN

accurate tie with the design. By doing so the orignal theme gets a distinctive spontaneity because a transfiguration takes place and the translation of vision and need of sensibility of the designer may originate within well-defined and flexible boundaries.
Remie de Cnodder

mesure qu'elle place ses laines, sans se limiter trop etroitement à l'esquisse. Ainsi, le theme initial acquiert une spontanéité particulaière par la transfiguration et la traduction, dans certains limites assez souples, de la vision et du besoin de sensibilitié de l'artiste.
Remi de Cnodder

Einbringen der Wollarten, das Bild organisch und ohne allzu eingehende Bindung mit dem Entwurf wachsen läszt. Auf diese Weise bekommt das originelle Thema eine besondere Spontaneitat, weil eine Umgestaltung stattfindet und die Übersetzung von Anschanuung und Bedürfnis nach Empfindlichkeit der Entwerferin innerhalb bestimmter geschmeidiger Grenzen entstehen kann.
Remi de Cnodder

BRENNAN

It's astonishing that the craft still survives today, and I know that I find particular delight in the required degreee of preplanning and the order of growth, slowly and erratically from one edge. Then there's the stuff about tapestry's special colour, texture, thread and rhythm. But all that is incidental, unless you are Penelope the work has to stand up on the wall.

I think I weave because there was a tapestry workshop near my family home; because I'm good at it; because I like making pictures; and because it's a slow, slow process. I quite like the epitaph—"He made relatively few mistakes in his career".

Il est surprenant que cet artisanat ait survécu jusqu'à nos jours. Pour ma part, je trouve du plaisir à me préparer étapes par étapes et à progresser dans mon ouvrage d'une manière lente et fantaisiste à partir d'une lisière. Il y a aussi la question de couleur particulière, de tissu, de fil et de rythme de la tapisserie. Mais tout cela n'est qu'accessoire car à moins que vous ne soyez Pénélope, on doit finir par accrocher la tapisserie au mur.

Je pense que je tisse parce qu'il avait un atelier de tissage près de chez moi, parce ce que j'ai du talent, parce que j'aime créer des images, parce que c'est un procédé très, très lent. J'aime assez cette épitaphe—"dans l'ensemble, il fit peu d'erreur dans sa carrière".

Es ist erstaunlich, dass dieses Gewerbe heutzutage noch überlebt. Ich weiss, dass ich besonderes Vergnügen daran habe, im richtigen Masse vorauszuplanen und die Entwicklung zu beobachten, die sich von einer Ecke langsam und sprunghaft bemerkbar macht. Und dann diese Sache mit der besonderen Farbe, der Textur, dem Faden und dem Rhythmus der Tapisserie. Aber all das ist rein zufällig—das Werk muss an der Wand stehen, es sei denn, man heisst Penelope.

Ich glaube, ich webe, weil es in meiner Nachbarschaft einmal einen Tapisserieworkshop gab, weil ich es gut kann, weil ich gerne Bilder entwerfe und weil es ein sehr langwieriger Prozess ist. Mir gefällt die Grabschrift—"Er hat während seiner Karriere relativ wenige Fehler gemacht".

FALKOWSKA

The fluttering leaves on the birch growing near the gate, the rain in the gutters, drops beating against a metal roof, through a window view a cranberry bush swayed by wind, the light on a stream. the scent of potato fields, the warmth of a sun-drenched rock.

Today these distant remembrances, sounds, scents, images are even more intense. They belong less to the objective world and are now mine. I carry them within and perpetuate their existence.

Perhaps it is a reason for our being—to carry on something of value?

The vertical, the horizontal and the sphere create the world. The vertical warp of life, the horizontal weft of thread impose their own rigors, which I respect and accept; yet I do not want to be dominated by them.

I seek the circle.

Le frémissement des feuilles du bouleau qui pousse près du portail, la pluie dans la gouttière, les gouttes d'eau tambourinant sur le toit métallique, le buisson de canneberge que le vent fait pencher, les reflets d'un ruisseau, l'odeur d'un champ de pommes de terre, la chaleur d'un rocher au soleil.

Voilà peut-être la notre raison d'être—la transmission de quelque chose de valeur.

Le monde est créé à partir de cercles et de lignes verticales et horizontales. La chaine verticale de la vie, la trame horizontale du fil imposent leurs règles propres: je les accepte et je les respecte mais je ne me laisse pas dominer.

Je suis à la recherche du cercle.

Die zitternden Birkenblätter bei der Pforte, der Regen im Rinnstein, fallende Tropfen auf einem Metalldach, ein vom Winde gewiegter Preiselbeerbusch, den man durch's Fenster erblickt, die Sonnenstrahlen auf einem Bach, der Geruch von Kartoffelfeldern, die Wärme eines sonnengebadeten Felsens.

Diese fernen Erinnerungen, Geräusche, Gerüche und Bilder werden heute sogar noch intensiver empfunden. Sie gehören immer weniger der objektiven Welt an und gehören nun mir allein. Ich trage sie in mir und lasse sie fortbestehen.

Vielleicht ist das ein Grund unseres Seins—etwas Wertvolles durch uns weiterbestehen zu lassen.

Die Vertikale, die Horizontale und die Kugel formen die Welt. Die vertikale Kette des Lebens und das horizontale Gewebe der Faser haben ihre eigenen Gesetze, die ich respektiere und akzeptiere, ich möchte jedoch nicht ihr Sklave sein.

Ich suche den Mittelpunkt.

GIBSON

clothing and architecture. The second source is from the traditional patterns of functional weaving such as twills and checks.

I weave in a slit-tapestry technique which allows me a spontaneity that enhances the graphic quality of my designs. Complementary to the graphic impact are the subtle variations in fibre, texture and colour that enhance the surface.

It is important for me that my work speaks equally of the heritage of weaving as well as the spiritual heritage of man's relationship with Nature.

tent leurs outils, leurs vêtements et leur architecture. Ensuite, je m'inspire des motifs traditionnels du tissage fonctionnel tels les lignes croisées et les damiers.

J'utilise la technique de tissage à fentes qui me laisse une plus grande spontanéité et relève la qualité graphique de mes dessins. Les variations subtiles des fibres, de la texture et de la couleur agrémentent la surface de la tapisserie et ajoutent à l'impression créée par le dessin.

Il est importamt que mon travail se réfère également à deux heritages: celui de la tapisserie et l'héritage spirituel des relations de l'homme avec la Nature.

die ihre Werkzeuge, Kleidung und Häuser zieren. Die zweite Quelle besteht aus den traditionellen Mustern des praktischen Webens, wie zum Beispiel Köperstoff und Karomuster.

Ich verwende beim Weben eine Schlitzmethode, die Spontanitat zur Betonung der graphischen Qualität meiner Entwürfe zulässt. Die bildliche Wirkung der Fläche wird durch die feinen Variationen in der Faser, im Muster und in der Farbe gesteigert.

Es ist mir wichtig, dass mein Werk zugleich die Entwicklung des Webens sowie die geistige Entwicklung der Beziehung zwischen Mensch und Natur ausdrückt.

GOLDSMITH

I like to surround myself with drawings, sketchbooks and objects and weave as spontaneously as possible using a palette of my own dyed yarns.

J'aime m'entourer de dessins, de cahier de croquis et d'objets et je tisse avec autant de spontanéité que possible en utilisant un assortiment de laines que je teins moi-même.

Très souvent, je peins par dessus les tapisseries qui sont finies car je trouve que le mélange de deux procédés si différents a quelque chose de passionnant.

Ich umgebe mich mit Zeichnungen, Skizzen, Malblocks und Objekten, und webe so spontan wie möglich mit einer Palette meiner selbstgefärbten Fasern.

Ich verwende oft den Siebdruck in meinen Werken—diese Kombination von zwei verschiedenen Medien begeistert mich.

KRAMER-PETERS

In realizing musical contents, forms, construction principals and, most of all, tonal reciprocations I am repeatedly inspired to new ways of presentation in the textile media, especially in the related matter of color. Working with color is always fascinating: to find the right color for an adequate expression and to compose mixtures and shadings offers a never ending variety of possibilities. This is, so to say, a compensation for the strictness of form and the weaving process.

L'appréhension du contenu, des formes, des principes de l'architecture musicale, et surtout des rapports réciproques entre tonalités est source intarissable d'inspirations qui débouchent sur de nouvelles voies de création, au travers des moyens d'expression propres au textile, notamment par le matériau couleur.

Ce jeu fascinant du travail de la couleur, cette recherche de l'expression exacte au travers de la sélection des composantes chromatiques, de leurs mariages et de leurs ombres, révèlent une richesse inépuisable de possiblités qui compensent, si l'on peut dire, la rigueur dictée par la forme et le tissage en soi.

Im Erkennen der musikalischen Inhalte, Formen, Bauprinzipien und vor allem der klanglichen Wechselwirkungen finden sich immer wieder Anregungen, die zu neuen Wegen der Darstellung mit textilen Ausdrucksmitteln führen, besonders in der verwandten Materie Farbe. Der immer wieder faszinierende Umgang mit der Farbe, die Suche nach adäquatem Ausdruck durch die Auswahl, das Herausfinden und Zusammenstellen von Mischungen und Schattierungen, bringt einen unerschöpflichen Reichtum an Möglichkeiten, sozusagen als Ausgleich für die Strenge, die durch die Form und den Webvorgang gegeben sind.

MAŃCZAK

The weaving process conceived in such terms has enabled me to present my photographic compositions for the second time — in different material and with the use of all those values and attributes that photography will never possess. I think that it would not be possible to achieve such results in technique other than weaving.

A fragment of reality registered with the use of the photographic technique and transposed into the language of tapestry becomes my individual interpretation of both photography and nature. The principle of arranging photographs into triptychs has enabled me to overcome all the limitations of the weaving process — and, what is more, has allowed to touch such vital problems as form and scale, the whole unit and its detail, valour and a type of material, etc. and has enabled me to present Nature as Sacred.

Cette technique de tissage m'a permis de représenter une deuxième fois mes créations photographiques — avec des matériaux différents et en utilisant toutes ces valeurs et attributs que la photographie ne possédera jamais. Je pense qu'il serait impossible d'obtenir les même resultats avec des techniques autres que celles du tissage.

J'interprète la photographie et la nature en photographiant des fragments de réalite avant de les transposer dans le language de la tapisserie. L'arrangement de mes photographies en triptyque me permet de surmonter les limitations de la technique de tissage — ainsi que de m'essayer aux problèmes essentiels de la forme et de l'échelle, de l'ouvrage dans son ensemble et dans ses détails, de la qualité et du genre des matériaux, etc. et enfin de rendre sensible le côté sacré de la Nature.

Diese Art des Webens bietet mir die Möglichkeit, meine photographischen Kompositionen neu zu interpretieren — in einem anderen Medium mit Hilfsmitteln und Farbwerten, die weder in der Photographie noch in anderen Medien existieren.

Ein Stück Wirklichkeit, das durch den photographischen Prozess eingefangen und in die Sprache des Webens übertragen wird, entwickelt sich in meine persönliche Interpretation der Photographie und der Natur. Dürch das Arrangieren von Photos in Triptychons kann ich uber die Grenzen des Webens hinausgehen — und vor allem kann ich mich mit Problemen befassen wie zum Beispiel Form und Maßstab, das Werk im Ganzen und im Detail, die Wahl des Materials etc. — es gibt mir die Möglichkeit, die Natur als heilige Natur zu vermitteln.

MAROIS

Abakanowiz, Jagoda Buit and Wojciech Sadley was growing stronger and I was fascinated by the energy, sensuality and intensity that came out of their works.

Having to place myself between the classical rigour of the woven image or the expressionism of the materials, the personalization of language became my primary motivation to create tapestries. My most important objective was to reconcile everything that already attracted me in the various orientations of modern tapestry at the time: rigour, atmosphere and expression.

Because I have always been aware of and preoccupied with different movements of contemporary Art, it is important for me to continue creating tapestries that subscribe to new aesthetics while keeping their classical and permanent character.

I find it important to keep on showing that tapestry can stay on the wall and remain contemporary, that the medium does not require complex surroundings nor special technical skills to prove its modernity and its total expressivity.

sion de la couleur. En même temps s'affirmait l'expressionisme de Magdalena Abakanowiz, Jagoda Buic et Wojciech Sadley qui me fascinait par son énergie, sa sensualité et l'atmosphère intense qui se dégageait de leurs oeuvres.

Avant de me définir entre la rigueur classique de l'image tissée ou l'expressionisme du materiaux, la personnalisation du langage devint pour moi ma principale stimulation à créer des tapisseries. Mon principal objectif était de réunir tout ce qui m'attirait déjà dans les différentes orientations de la tapissserie contemporaine de cette époque, c'est-à-dire, la rigueur, l'atmosphère et l'expression.

Ayant toujours été attentif et preóccupe par les différents mouvements de l'Art actuel, il est important pour moi de continuer à créer des tapisseries qui s'inscrivent dans les nouvelles ésthetiques tout en conservant leur caractère classique et permanent.

Il est important pour moi de continuer à prouver que la tapisserie peut demeurer au mur et être actuelle, que le meduim n'a pas besoin de mises en scènes complexes de l'installation et de trop de démonstration technique pour témoigner de sa modernité et de sa totale passivité.

derselben Zeit verstärkte sich auch die Ausdruckskraft von Magdalena Abakanowiz, Jagoda Buic und Wojciech Sadley. Ich war fasziniert von der Energie, Sinnlichkeit und Intensität, die ihre Werke ausstrahlten.

Ich stand also gewissermassen in der Mitte zwischen der klassischen Strenge des gewebten Motivs und der Ausdruckskraft der verschiedenen Materialien. Daraus ergab sich als meine Hauptaufgabe im Entwerfen von Tapisserien die Illustration der Sprache. Mein wichtigstes Ziel war, alles, was mich bisher an den modernen Stilrichtungen gereizt hatte, zu vereinigen: Disziplin, Atmosphäre und Ausdruckskraft.

Ich war schon immer an den verschiedenen modernen Kunstrichtungen interessiert, und so ist es mir wichtig, weiterhin Tapisserien zu entwerfen, die eine neue Ästhetik ausdrücken und trotzdem ihren klassischen und permanenten Charakter bewahren. Es ist mir wesentlich zu zeigen, dass die Tapisserie an der Wand hängen und aktuell bleiben kann, dass das Medium keine komplexe Installation braucht oder besondere Fähigkeiten benötigt, um zu beweisen, wie zeitgemäss und ausdrucksvoll es sein kann.

MILLS

I feel privileged to be a part of the chain (that preceded the making of paper or canvas) which links the Coptic and pre-Columbian tapestries and includes desert nomads and William Morris.

My work continues to be mainly about the human condition and the devices required for trying to stay upright.

les choses qui importent dans la vie—telle la tapisserie.

J'ai le privilège d'être un des anneaux de la chaine (qui précède la fabrication du papier et de la toile) qui relie les tapisseries Coptes aux tapisseries pré-Colombiennes sans oublier les nomades et William Morris.

Dans mon travail, je m'occupe principalement de la condition de l'homme et de tout ce qui lui est nécessaire pour garder la station debout.

Ich fühle mich geehrt, einer Kette (die schon vor der Papier-und Leinwanderzeugung existierte) anzugehören, die koptische und vorkolumbianische Wandteppiche verbindet, und der auch die Wüstennomaden und William Morris angehören.

Mein Werk befasst sich weiterhin hauptsächlich mit menschlichen Verhältnissen und den Mitteln, die zum Überleben notwendig sind.

NAGY

If I weave and embroider them with the finely painted wool-thread and spun-silk, the "bug-colours" thereof growing together by the rolling years—I perhaps save some of them for the distant future.

A gobelin woven with love is just like a fragile insect—single and irreproducible.

I like to sit down at the loom every day and to stroke the finely painted wool-thread and spun-silk. To blend the shades of colour and to imagine what will become of them. It is fine to go to bed in the evening knowing that the warped gobelin has grown today by some centimetres, it will grow tomorrow again and will perhaps be completed in one or two months. Then comes the ironing with the sweet-smell of the drying wool. The excitement—has it succeeded?—is it like I expected it to be?—when to begin the next one?

Perhaps, one of my woven children will get a place where someone will notice the love woven therein, the patient impatience and the message sent to him.

En tissant et en brodant ces "insectes colores" avec des fils de laine et des fils de soie de teintes délicates, j'en protège peut-être quelques uns d'un futur distant.

Un gobelin tissé avec amour est comme un insecte fragile—unique et irremplaçable.

J'ai plaisir à m'asseoir à mon métier à tisser tous les jours, à caresser mes précieux échevaux de laine et de soie, à mélanger les tons et à m'imaginer ce qu'ils donneront. J'aime me coucher le soir sachant que mon gobelin a avancé de quelques centimètres aujourd'hui, qu'il progressera demain aussi et qu'il sera peut-etre fini dans un ou deux mois. J'aime aussi l'odeur douce de la laine qui sèche quand je le repasse et l'excitement qui suit—l'ai-je réussi?—est-ce ce que je le voulais ainsi?—quand vais-je en commencer un autre?

Un jour peut-être, l'un des mes enfants tissés se trouvera dans un endroit où quelqu'un remarquera l'amour qui est brodé en lui, la patiente impatience et le message que je lui envoie.

Indem ich sie mit bemaltem Wollgarn und gesponnener Seide in ihren "Insektenfarben" webe und besticke, kann ich vielleicht einige von ihnen für die ferne Zukunft bewahren.

Ein mit Liebe gewebter Wandteppich ist wie ein zerbrechliches Insekt—einzigartig und unnachahmbar.

Ich sitze gerne jeden Tag am Webstuhl und streiche mit den Händen über die feinbemalten Woll-und Seidenfäden. Ich denke darüber nach, wie ich die Farbschattierungen zustande bringen könnte und ich stelle mir vor, wie es am Ende aussehen könnte. Es ist ein gutes Gefühl, abends mit der Gewissheit zu Bett zu gehen, dass der Gobelin um einige Zentimeter gewachsen ist und dass er am nächsten Tag weiterwächst und vielleicht in ein oder zwei Monaten vollendet sein wird. Dann kommt das Bügeln mit dem süssen Duft von trocknender Wolle. Die Aufregung—ist es gelungen? Entspricht es meinen Erwartungen? Wann beginne ich mit dem Nächsten?

Vielleicht wird eines meiner gewebten "Kinder" einen Tages einen Platz finden, wo man die hineingewebte Liebe, die geduldige Ungeduld und die darin enthaltene Botschaft erkennt.

PAINTER

Once the addiction set in, which was quickly, there was a strong driving force: perpetual, consuming, and sometimes even rewarding.

The art form also needs a strong dedication to obscurity for years of developing technique, confidence, and need I say, a market.

I only wish I could weave more and more and not be distracted by the day to day necessaries.

Apres m'être rapidement adonné à cet art, je me suis senti poussé par une force perpétuelle, dévorante et parfois même rémunératrice.

Cette forme d'Art nécessite une dédication absolue pendant les premières années obscures où l'on developpe sa technique et sa maitrise et a besoin bien entendu d'un marché.

Maintenant je souhaiterais tisser de plus en plus sans être interrompu par les nécessités de la vie de tous les jours.

Ich war von Anfang an fasziniert—eine kräftige Macht hatte mich ergriffen, die beständig, verzehrend und manchmal befriedigend war.

Diese Kunstform verlangt Hingabe und Verdammung zur Einsamkeit in den Jahren, in denen man die Methode verfeinert, Selbstvertrauen gewinnt und einen Kundenkreis aufbaut.

Ich wünsche nur, ich hätte mehr Zeit zum Weben und wäre nicht so sehr von meinen täglichen Verantwortungen abgelenkt.

SAWYER

I love the idea of weaving—the design and the structure being so integrated. I enjoy creating three dimensional forms, using basically simple elements—verticals, diagonals, etc.; easy to construct, but offering immense imaginative scope.

"The Architecture Shop" developed from a fantasy about choosing a new place to live. Order a miniature temple, perhaps, or terraced housing by the metre . . . .

J'aime l'idée de tisser—le dessin et la structure étant tellement intégrés. J'ai plaisir à créer des formes à trois dimensions en utilisant des éléments relativement simples—des verticales, des diagonales etc; la construction en est facile mais cela laisse le champ totalement libre à l'imagination.

'L'Atelier d'Architecture' est le résultat d'un fantasme que j'avais pour choisir une nouvelle demeure: commander un temple miniature peut-etre ou des rangées de maisons au mètre . . .

Ich liebe die Idee des Webens—die Integration des Designs mit der Struktur. Ich entwerfe gerne dreidimensionale Formen mit einfachen Elementen—Vertikale, Diagonale etc; eben Formen, die leicht zu konstruieren sind, die jedoch einen Spielraum von ungeheurer Grösse bieten.

"The Architecture Shop" (das Architekturgeschäft) entsprang dem Wunsch, an einem neuen Ort zu leben. Man bestellt einen Miniaturtempel, vielleicht, oder ein Haus mit Terrasse nach Metermass . . . .

SCHUSTER

concept of male and female. Traditionally, each element has been assigned opposing characteristics such as positive/negative, active/passive and warm/cool.

In my work the duality theme is conveyed in two ways: by the superimposition of figurative images which remain physically separate yet merge visually, and by the interaction of color with abstract linear elements in order to create spatial illusions. These two methods of expression are in themselves representative of the duality theme.

yang exprime cette dualité d'une manière symbolique alors que les concepts mâles et femelles expriment cette même dualité d'une manière métaphorique. Selon une certaine tradition, on a donné à chaque élément des caractéristiques opposées: positif/négatif, actif/passif et chaud/froid.

Je transmets cette idée de dualité de deux manières dans mon travail: je superpose des images métaphoriques qui restent séparées tout en se fondant visuellement et je mélange les couleurs avec des éléments linéaires abstraits afin de créer une illusion spaciale. Ces deux moyens d'expression contiennent en euxmêmes le thème de la dualité.

ausgedrückt, und metaphorisch durch den Begriff von männlich und weiblich. Jedem Element sind bestimmte gegensätzliche Eigenschaften zugeordnet: positiv/negativ, aktiv/passiv und warm/kalt.

In meiner Arbeit wird das Thema Dualität auf zweierlei Weise verdeutlicht: durch das Übereinanderschichten von bildlichen Motiven, die separat sind, jedoch visuell zusammenschmelzen—und durch die Wechselwirkung der Farbe mit abstrakten linearen Elementen, um räumliche Illusionen zu erwecken. Diese beiden Ausdrucksmittel sind in sich selbst ein Thema der Dualität.

STINSON

linen, brushed mohair, and metallic threads, as well as the more usual worsted. The images are sometimes representational, but often purely abstract. "Yellow Wall Piece" is one of several tapestries which have been inspired by marks made on walls: prehistoric cave paintings, hieroglyphics, caligraphic marks and graffiti.

variées pour differencier les surfaces multiples du papier. Je me sers de soie, de coton, de lin, de laine mohair, de fils métalliques et aussi des laines peignees plus communes. Les images sont parfois figuratives mais le plus souvent elles sont purement abstraites. "Pan de Mur Jaune" est une des tapisseries qui ont tiré leur inspiration de marques faites sur des murs: peintures rupestres, hiéroglyphes, inscriptions caligraphiques et graffiti.

gerne verschiedenartige Fasern, um die verschiedenen Papieroberflächen wiederzugeben. Unter anderem verwende ich Seide, Baumwolle, Leinen, gekämmte Angorawolle, Metallfäden sowie gewöhnliches Kammgarn. Die Motive sind manchmal gegenständlich, oft aber auch rein abstrakt. "Yellow Wall Piece" (gelber Wandbehang) ist eins von vielen Tapisserien, die durch Wandmarkierungen inspiriert wurden: vorgeschichtliche Höhlenwandmalerei, Hieroglyphen, kalligraphische Schriftzeichen und Graffiti.

SZARAZ

The rigidity of a traditional technique reminds me of transmitted traditions and the image reflects contemporary impressions. I combine a relatively simple composition with a layering technique. That apparent simplicity does not imply poor expressiveness. It serves two purposes: the viewer must focus his attention on the messages transmitted by all the details (material, technique, colors) so that he can participate and open up to the tapestry.

"paraitre" la vie extériorisée vue dans la famille. Les mots "cacher" et "protéger" se confondent, deviennent le symbole du vécu antérieur.

La rigueur de la technique traditionnelle rappelle pour moi les traditions transmises, et l'image est le reflet des impressions d'aujourd'hui. A côté de la composition relativement simple, j'utilise les superpositions. Cette simplicité apparente ne signifie pas pauvreté d'expression mais invitation d'une part à se concentrer uniquement sur les messages qui se dégagent de tous les détails (matière, technique, couleurs) et d'autre part, à provoquer une ouverture et une participation des spectateurs.

tecken" und "beschützen" überschneiden und verschmelzen sich zu einem erlebten Symbol.

Die Strenge der herkömmlichen Methode erinnert mich an übertragene Traditionen. Das Motiv ist ein Spiegel aktueller Impressionen. Ich verbinde eine relativ einfache Komposition mit einer Schichtungsmethode. Diese scheinbare Einfachheit ist aber nicht identisch mit mangelhafter Ausdruckskraft. Sie dient folgendem Zweck: der Betrachter soll auf die Botschaft, die in den Details (Material, Ausführung, Farbe) enthalten ist, aufmerksam werden, so dass er am Werk teilhaben kann und ihm aufgeschlossen ist.

TYRELL

Although very different from my large woven landscapes (which are usually perceived as peaceful) they continue my interest in finding memorable images in tapestry that seek to evoke an emotional response from the viewer.

ristes, des ralliements du Ku Klux Klan et des scènes de guerre et de destruction.

Bien qu'elles soient très differentes des larges tapisseries où je décris des paysages (qui reflètent un certain calme), elles me fascinent car elles m'obligent à trouver des images inoubliables qui frappent le spectateur.

tierten Flugzeugen, brennenden Öltankern, Terroristen, Ku Klux Klan Kundgebungen und Szenen des Krieges und der Zerstörung.

Obwohl die Wandteppiche sich von meinen grossen gewebten Landschaften (die normalerweise als friedlich gelten) unterscheiden, bestärken sie weiterhin mein Interesse an der Suche nach bedeutungsvollen Motiven, die eine Gefühlsregung im Betrachter auslösen sollen.

WUSTINGER

keep them in the background. The relationship of the colors to each other should develop as smoothly as possible. I give in to the colors, their needs, and they become cheerful. "Sahara 2" was created after a journey to the Sahara desert. I recognized the Sahara, or rather my feelings about the Sahara, in the completed tapestry. Of course, I don't know which deserts the viewers have visited . . .

nait, se rappelle à nous dans le travail même. Je choisis des fondations légères que je garde à l'arrière-plan. Les rapports entre les couleurs devraient se coordonner aussi facilement que possible. Je m'abandonne aux couleurs, à leurs besoins, et elles deviennnent gaies. J'ai créé "Sahara 2" à mon retour du Sahara. J'ai reconnu le Sahara, ou plutôt ce que je ressentais pour le Sahara, dans la tapisserie finie. Bien entendu, je ne sais pas quel désert les spectateurs ont exploré . . .

Fonds, damit sie nicht vordergründig werden. Die Beziehungen der Farben zueinander sollen sich möglichst ungestört entwickeln. Ich gebe den Farben, ihrem Verlangen nach, und sie werden heiter. "Sahara 2" entstand nach einem Sahara-Aufenthalt. Im fertigen Gobelin erkannte ich die Sahara, also meine Empfindungen ihr gegenüber wieder. Natürlich weiss ich nicht, in welchen Wüsten die Betrachter waren . . .

ZIEGLER

This place is known as the "Hall of the lost steps" and I changed it to the "Hall of the lost years." Referring to the political period during which democracy was abolished in my country.

Technically I found that the greatest difficulty was the symmetry when weaving on the weft direction, but the original idea was still alive and the work was finished.

Cette partie du Palais est connue comme la "Sala de los pasos perdidos" (Salle des pas perdus), et j'ai changé le nom de l'ouvrage à *Salle des annees perdues*, en taisant allusion aux années pendant lesquelles la democratie a été supprimée.

Du point de vue technique, j'ai trouvé la principale difficulté dans la symétrie du tissage dans le sens de la trame, mais l'idee originale était vivante et l'ouvrage a été terminé.

Der erwähnte Platz ist als "Halle der verlorenen Schritte" bei uns bekannt. Ich änderte den Begriff und verwandelte ihn in die "Halle der verlorenen Jahre", in Bezug auf unsere politische Wirklichkeit, in der die Demokratie abgeschaffen war.

Im technischen Bereich musste ich die Schwierigkeit überwinden, die gewebte Symmetrie bis zum Schluss zu wahren.

ACKNOWLEDGEMENTS

This catalogue has been made possible in part by the generous gifts from the Australia Council; Blue Ridge Foundation, Inc.; City of Chicago Department of Cultural Affairs, Office of Fine Arts; H. D. Ellis; C. F. Giuliano; Jewish Communal Fund of New York; the Victorian Ministry for the Arts, Victoria, Australia and members of the American Tapestry Alliance.

We are pleased to acknowledge the support of Continental Airlines as the "official carrier" for the conferees of "Tapestry Today" in Melbourne and Chicago's "Convergence 88" sponsored by the Handweavers Guild of America.

We and the artists are exceedingly grateful to Don Newman and Continental Airlines for transporting the exhibition.

Special thanks go to Laurie Kosky and her great staff from the North Shore Weavers Guild as hosts of "Convergence 88" and Gregory Knight, Director of Visual Arts, Chicago Office of Fine Arts, the Cultural Center and staff for all their assistance in helping make Chicago a focal point for tapestry.

Sue Walker's (Director of the Victorian Tapestry Workshop) collaborative efforts in this exhibition gave much impetus in making this a truly international exhibit. Her staff deserve much credit and in particular my special thanks to Carloyn Whip for all her efforts. We are most grateful to Clinton Greenwood and his staff at the Meat Market Craft Centre for their care in the installation there.

The efforts of Diane Bell for the Bell•Ross Gallery in Memphis and Ann Cooper for the Scheuer Tapestry Gallery in New York are particularly appreciated. Herr Schubert, Textilmuseum Berk, Heidelberg; Frau Dr. Sedelmeier, Office of Cultural Events, City Hall, Stuttgart, both of Germany; and Martine Mathais, Musée departemental de la tapisserie, Centre Culturel et Artistique Jean Lurçat; and Paul Risch, Ecole Nationale d'Art Decoratif d'Aubusson, have been most helpful in arranging the European venues in Germany and France.

I extend sincere personal thanks to Ruth Myers, Sally Schoch and Jane Hartford for their encouragement for this project to be part of Handweavers Guild of America's Convergence 88 and to John Vedel-Rieper, Secretary General, World Crafts Coucil for his cooperation and to the World Craft Council national entities.

And lastly, Joy Rushfelt, may she renew her interest in tapestry; Helga Berry and Walter Harris for their in-house translations; Tara Torburn for her loyalty to this project; Steve Hill and Steve Werner's patience in the typesetting; John Bell's understanding and perfectionism in publishing; Larry Knowles and the American Tapestry Alliance board of directors, Ruth Scheuer, Hal Painter, Nancy Harvey and Muriel Nehznie for the extraordinary efforts they made toward the successful conclusion of this project.

Typeset: Central Graphics, San Diego, California
Layout: Tara Lee Torburn, Oceanside, California
Printer: The Ovid Bell Press, Fulton, Missouri
Translations: Trans-Laangg, San Diego, California

The American Tapestry Alliance is a non-profit corporation founded to promote tapestry and its makers. Contributions are welcome and are tax deductible to the extent allowed by law. For further information about the works or artists in this catalogue, or membership information write: American Tapestry Alliance, HC 63 Box 570-D Chiloquin, OR 97624 USA